HANDBOOK TO HAPPINESS
And YOU

A Spiritual Clinic

WITHDRAWN

HANDBOOK TO HAPPINESS
And YOU

A Spiritual Clinic

Charles R. Solomon, Ed. D.

Exchanged Life Foundation
Publisher
Denver, Colorado

132812

Dedication

To my mother who still prays for me at 87; friends who have encouraged, prayed, and sacrificially supported God's work at Grace Fellowship International (GFI); and to the staff and board members, past and present, who have poured out their lives that the message of the cross might be proclaimed to a hurting world.

Library of Congress Catalog Card Number 91-077458

Exchanged Life Foundation, Publisher
P. O. Box 27315
Denver, CO 80227

First Edition 1991

Cover painting and sketches by Nikolo Balkanski
The works of Nikolo Balkanski, an accomplished internationally recognized artist, have hung in places of national honor in a number of European countries and the United States. His love of nature has prompted Balkanski to become a landscape artist as well as a portrait artist. He now maintains his studio and permanent residence in Lakewood, Colorado.

PSALM 107:23-31

They that go down to the sea in ships, that do business in great waters; These see the works of the Lord, and his wonders in the deep. For he commandeth, and raiseth the stormy wind, which lifteth up the waves thereof. They mount up to the heaven, they go down again to the depths: their soul is melted because of trouble. They reel to and fro, and stagger like a drunken man, and are at their wit's end. Then they cry unto the lord in their trouble, and he bringeth them out of their distresses. He maketh the storm a calm, so that the waves thereof are still. Then are they glad because they be quiet; so he bringeth them unto their desired haven. Oh that men would praise the Lord for his goodness, and for his wonderful works to the children of men!

Preface
Foreword

PART I

A PERSONAL SPIRITUAL CLINIC
17

PART II

A SPIRITUAL CLINIC FOR YOUR CHURCH
75

PREFACE

This book is written to those who are hurting and/or their loved ones, neither of whom may know where to turn for resolution of long-standing problems. Many have been referred to the fields of psychology and psychiatry only to be disappointed with the results after major outlays of funds and wasted time. The author knows of a pastor whose son was hospitalized, and he and the insurance company (mostly, the insurance company) paid out more than $400,000 to no avail. A lady (in conjunction with her insurance) had paid out more than $1,000,000 before finding the only complete answer in the Lord Jesus Christ. The lady who counseled with her had less than 3 months of training, but God used her in sharing truth from His Word literally to transform her life. Multiplied millions of dollars of the Lord's money find their way into the coffers of the world system yearly—money spent on cisterns (and theories) which do not hold water. "For my people have committed two evils; they have forsaken me the fountain of living waters, and hewed them out cisterns, broken cisterns, that can hold no water." (Jer. 2:13)

The PERSONAL SPIRITUAL CLINIC will allow you to have a counseling session with Dr. Solomon by proxy using the material normally covered in the initial interview. Over the past two decades, God has used

Handbook to Happiness to explain the scriptures without the benefit of a counselor, and the Holy Spirit has miraculously changed (or exchanged) innumerable lives. As you approach such a study, do so with an open Bible, an open mind and a prayerful spirit. Everything taught in this book could and should be made available in the average local church by the rank and file church member.

This being the case, PART II is addressed to the church but more to the average believer than to professional Christians. Though it has been my desire to work closely with church leadership, those holding the reins in the Christian establishment have been less than cordial to a counseling/discipleship emphasis which makes the Cross (Gal. 2:20) central and the message of grace paramount. However, maintaining this stance will be increasingly difficult as lives, families, and society continue to come unglued.

In many ways the modern church has defaulted on its God-given mandate to equip the saints for the work of the ministry, for the edifying of the body of Christ (Eph. 4:12). The emphasis has been on a clergy/laity division which is unscriptural and which forces the majority of believers to take a spectator role. This is in clear violation of the priesthood of the believer where each should exercise his spiritual gifts in ministry. Only as each member of the Body of Christ carries out his (her) function will the defeated or impotent church become the church triumphant.

Evangelism has fallen short of the mark in that proper emphasis has been placed on forgiveness of sins and the new birth, but too little on losing the old life in exchange for the new. Discipleship has taken a decided back seat to evangelism with the force of the Great Commission in the average church being more on *going* and *doing* than on *teaching* and *being*. Absent

8

the teaching of the Cross and the exchanged life, discipleship degenerates into disciplining the flesh or self-centered life to comply with scriptural injunctions. And, yet, Luke 14:27 states: "And whosoever doth not bear his cross and come after me, cannot be my disciple."

The corrective measures so desperately needed in the church must begin with the individual believer coming to know his identity in Christ "That the man of God may be perfect (mature), throughly furnished unto all good works" (2 Tim. 3:17). The Personal Spiritual Clinic is designed to assist you in assessing your spiritual maturity and to find in the Lord Jesus Christ all that you need to walk with Him in victory and become spiritually effective. Then, it will be possible for you to take your place as a minister in the body, utilizing the spiritual gifts with which He has equipped you. After a while, it will become very simple for you to walk someone through the Spiritual Clinic and see the Holy Spirit absolutely transform the life.

It is my prayer that each of us will yield to the Lord Jesus Christ that He may be our all in all and that we may function as His Body as He intended, "That he might present it to himself a glorious church, not having spot, or wrinkle, or any such thing; but that it should be holy and without blemish." (Eph. 5:27)

The Author

FOREWORD

The name of Charles Solomon is increasingly mentioned in evangelical circles in this country today when the conversation turns to methods of counseling and especially to Christian counseling. He has many supporters who acclaim his methods as superior to all other counseling approaches and as the only, or at least one of the few approaches, which stands solidly on the foundation of the inerrant Word. At the same time will be found his critics who decry his approach saying that he merely spiritualizes psychological problems and that he has nothing in the way of healing to offer those who are mentally and emotionally distraught. It is also true to say that most of those in the opposition camp represent the professional communities of the behavioral sciences, namely, psychiatry, psychotherapy, and psychology.

How is it, then, that I, as a practicing psychiatrist and psychoanalyst in the rather classical Freudian tradition, can write an introduction and recommendation for Dr. Solomon's latest book? The answer is quite simple. In all of my thirty years as a Psychiatrist and Professional Therapist, I do not believe that I have ever met a counselor of any breed or variety who personally is more Christ-like or more committed to the inspired Word than Charles Solomon. It is for this reason that I have very little patience with those Christian professionals who degenerate to the level of the *ad hominem* when discussing Dr. Solomon's work and ideas, and who inaccurately, inappropriately and, sometimes, mendaciously accuse him of promulgating erroneous theological views which may even be heretical in nature. Charles Solomon stands squarely on the foundation of the inerrant and inspired Word; and no one's faith in that Word, or the Christ whom it presents, will ever be subverted by reading his works.

This is not to say that from a professional point of view I would agree with all of Solomon's ideas or with everything that he has ever written. I do, however, sufficiently respect him as a Christian and a colleague that I can discuss our differences together in an amicable fashion and in a way in which, I am hopeful, we can both learn from each other. I have always found it to be healthy, on finding someone with whom or something with which I disagree, to remember that I might be wrong. Out of such an attitude comes the constant desire and willingness to learn. I am happy to say I have learned from Charles Solomon.

As a rather classical psychiatrist and psycho-analyst, I have a model of mental functioning and psychopathology which emphasizes developmental and unconscious factors. This does not mean that in any sense I minimize the spiritual dimension. I have, however, found it to be a sad fact that individuals who suffer from essential psychological difficulties sometimes have a difficult time appropriating theological truth to themselves and their own situation. Every therapist who claims to be Christian has had the experience of working with individuals who have frequently been told to "give the problem to Jesus". However, there has not been a sufficient recognition that the individual's ability to "give" such a problem to anyone is defective, perhaps because of their very psychopathology. The severe ambivalence of the schizophrenic patient or of the obsessive-compulsive patient often will, itself, be an insurmountable barrier to belief and healing.

I believe that there are reasons why Dr. Solomon's work is not just rejected by the majority of the counseling profession but is actually unwanted by the majority in the evangelical church. In my opinion it is because he presents a message of the need for personal sanctification and "the Cross" which is not popular in today's narcissistic and hedonistic society and which few people want to hear. It is the old question of "the offense of the Cross" (Galatians 5:11). People today, and not just patients, would much prefer to think of their difficulties in terms of developmental factors, such as their relationship with their mother in the first few years of life, than to confront their own narcissism, selfishness, egocentricity, and reluctance to accept personal responsibility for their own life and functioning, whether physical, psychological, or spiritual.

Dr. Solomon correctly teaches us that happiness is far from being a mere choice, but is rather related to our willingness to be "set apart" or sanctified, so that we find our homeostasis, security, and happiness in Christ. This involves, however, self-denial and the repudiation of the old nature with all its selfish wants and desires. Even if an individual should suffer from a classical psychological or psychiatric difficulty or even from a physically-based problem, such submission to the headship of Christ remains for the Christian the mandatory and only foundation on which true happiness can be built.

Dr. Solomon, in his renewed emphasis on the Spirit-filled life and sanctification counseling has done the church a great service, in that he has reminded us of our spiritual heritage, and of issues which must be confronted and dealt with in the life of the believer who seeks homeostasis and health. I remain convinced that if this were to be preached and practiced in the church today, we would need fewer "behavioral scientists" or the current plethora of inadequately trained "Christian Therapists" or the schools in which they receive such inadequate training. When psychology and counseling is made a substitute for "The Cross" and the soul-searching work of the Holy Spirit, the church is in trouble. Dr. Solomon has reminded us of this, and we stand in his debt.

Basil Jackson, M.D., Ph. D., Th. D.
Medical Director
Department of Mental Health
St. Francis Hospital
Milwaukee, WI

Meet Dr. Solomon...

PART I
A Spiritual Clinic

THE PATH TO
SPIRITUAL MATURITY–
A Guided Tour

The spiritual birth is merely the beginning of a journey toward maturity which is only perfected when we see our Lord face to face. On any journey, it is vital that we know the destination; but it is very helpful if we have some milestones along the way to assess our direction and progress toward that goal. Many believers just muddle along all of their lives and do not know that they can appropriate by faith the Lord Jesus Christ as their very life. As a result, they live their whole life in the strength of the flesh with many doing yeoman's service and yet falling short of the victory that the Holy Spirit is ready to give to each and every believer. Too many who find the abundant life do so by trial and error and only after sustaining much damage and defeat in their own lives and, usually, passing along their problems to those whom they love.

The purpose of the PERSONAL SPIRITUAL CLINIC is to assist you in walking through your life from the beginning to attain an understanding of how your self-concept was developed (or how your flesh was programmed), an understanding of what it means to be in Christ, and how the exchange may be made from one to the other. Once you have made this discovery by the illumination of the Holy Spirit, He can use you to do the same with others in discipling them individually or in sharing with a group. Since it is spiritual ministry, it is not necessary to have formal training to be used of God in pointing those who are defeated and hurting to victory or abundant life in the Lord Jesus Christ.

While the behavioral sciences attempt to make a diagnosis of the problem in order to determine the pathology and a course of treatment or therapy, it is symptoms that are being addressed almost without exception. Unless therapists have dealt with the flesh or self-centered life in their own experience, they will stop short of seeing this as the root problem in anyone else. Therefore, their treatment of symptoms, if successful, will exacerbate the *problem*–the self-life. When the self-life or flesh is assisted in functioning at a higher (?) level, it merely delays the person's coming to the end of his own resources that he might live in the limitless resources of the Lord Jesus Christ.

In Spirituotherapy® (a word coined to denote the Christ-centered counseling pioneered by GFI), the goal is to help the individual understand the self-defeating identity out of which he is living and how he may deny this identity (Luke 9:23) and lose his life (Matt. 16;24,25; John 12:24,25) in order to live out of his new, and true, identity, ". . . Christ in you the hope of glory". (Col. 1:27b).

I. BACKGROUND INFORMATION

Securing a systematic life history has proven extremely beneficial in fostering self-understanding. Uncovering the rejection patterns, trauma, sin and other self-defeating, if not sinful, patterns of living and relating to others can make sense out of otherwise mysterious behavior and emotional instability. The typical interview would elicit such a history prior to offering a scriptural answer to the dilemma in which the person finds himself. The purpose is to help him understand why he feels, thinks, and behaves the way he does. Or, to put it another way, why is the flesh programmed in a particular direction? While understanding it in no way justifies it, there are usually some very rational explanations for irrational, if not sinful behavior. Once the flesh is isolated as the culprit, it is possible to go on to show how the Cross is the only complete answer to dealing with it; dealing with anything short of the flesh, even assiduous confession and repentance of sin, is but to treat symptoms rather than the problem. In God's economy, only a new life or revival will suffice; *dealing with the out-croppings of the flesh will merely result in a new crop of the same or another variety–sometimes a strain more resistant to the Spirit than the original!*

Such a life history makes it possible to evaluate the present conflict in light of antecedent events and gain an understanding of the person, not just his behavior in a particular set of circumstances. Once that identity has been established, it can be wrapped up with a nice black ribbon, appropriate for burial, and exchanged for the new life in Christ; this new life is a life out of death, revival, or the filling of the Holy Spirit, depending upon your choice of terms for the person's entering into the abundant life (John 10:10).

Prior to assessing your life history or that of someone else, it will be extremely helpful for you to have read through page 107 of *The Ins and Out of Rejection* and the first two chapters of *The Rejection Syndrome* by the author. This will prepare you to understand the entire fabric of the life, not just some threads, snarls and tangles here and there.

Over the past 20 years, the following questions have been found to be extremely helpful in eliciting a life history and can be done personally or by asking them of another person. If done in an informal or group setting with both men and women, it is suggested that questions of a sexual nature be omitted to avoid embarrassment and the possibility of betrayal of confidentiality. If the person wishes to volunteer something, it is his responsibility if that information is not used responsibly by someone who is merely a participant and not an authorized discipler or counselor. *In any relationship, confidential information is to be treated as a sacred trust.*

With all of that in mind, let's proceed with the questions. It will be helpful if you will write down the answers to the questions in the book or on a separate piece of paper concerning yourself or the one you are discipling for future reference. Discipling should *always* be on a same sex basis; this makes it possible to ask those questions of a private nature, individually, so that nothing is omitted which has a bearing on the life and that discipleship may continue on a deep level of friendship without the temptation of romantic involvement.

Please spend some time in prayer for insight given by the Holy Spirit as you take this solo journey through your past. He can bring to mind forgotten or repressed events and give you understanding and grace to deal with that which will bring healing and freedom from long-standing conflicts.

LIFE HISTORY–The Intake Interview

1. Are your parents living?
2. If so, are they living together?
3. If one or both died or they are separated,
   what age were you at the time?
4. If such changes took place, where or with whom
   did you live afterward?
5. Was this the only marriage for your parents?
6. How many siblings (brothers and sisters) in your
   immediate family? Where do you fit in? How
   many years difference between you and those
   siblings immediately younger and older?
7. If a stepparent were involved, how were you
   treated? Compare your treatment with that of
   stepbrothers and stepsisters by the stepparent.
8. If you had to leave the parental home, what was
   your living situation? How did you feel about it?
   Were one or all siblings with you?
9. As a child, were you closer to your mom or to your
   dad? Which could you talk to about threatening
   matters, if either?
10. Did either parent express or show love?
11. Was favoritism shown to other siblings?
12. Do you vividly recall any significant happenings–
    bad or good–prior to beginning school?
13. Were you ever sexually molested? At what age?
    By same sex or opposite sex? Someone your age or
    adult? Did you ever tell anyone about it? How
    long after it occurred?
14. How did you relate to siblings?
    Was there jealousy?
15. Were either or both of your parents
    overprotective? Describe.
16. From the ages of 6 to 12, were you outgoing?
    Withdrawn? Happy? Sad?

17. How many close friends from ages 6 to 12?
18. Were there any significant changes in your attitudes toward yourself or others during junior high school? Significant events?
19. What were you like during high school? When did you start dating? Any steadies?
20. What about sexual development and relationships during high school? Same or opposite sex? Guilt over self-stimulation?
21. Did you complete high school?
22. What did you do after high school? College? Military service? Any combat? Work?
23. At what age were you married? Children? If that marriage failed, at what age? Subsequent marriages? Children and/or stepchildren?
24. Describe the marriage(s).
25. What kind of work or study are you in at present?
26. What is your emotional and mental state at the present time? Any physiological symptoms?
27. Have you ever been in therapy? When? What kind? How long? Prescribed drugs at present?
28. Any problems, past or present, with drugs or alcohol? Any occult involvement?
29. If married, how is sexual adjustment?
30. Are there any excessive financial pressures at this time? Do you and spouse agree on money management?
31. Describe communication with spouse.
33. Do you have a relationship with God? How established? At what age? Are you currently affiliated with a church? What kind? Are you regular in attendance? Active in ministry?
34. What do you see as the chief problem which must be resolved?
35. Do you believe you are open to God's solution?

Once the history has been completed, it should be summarized in terms of identity such that the individual trees do not obscure the forest! This can be done by assessing the operation of the rejection syndrome, how this has affected the emotional state, and how it eventuates in certain types of behavior. The summary of rejection and its results contained on pages 79-84 of *Counseling with the Mind of Christ* by the author (remaining copies available at GFI) will be helpful in pulling together its effects in an understandable fashion. One who has been rejected will reject himself in some aspects of his personality and will, in turn, reject others if only by preventing them from getting close to him. Plans and goals may have been thwarted by self-rejection and a tendency to shoot oneself out of the saddle, since success would be inconsistent with feelings of failure.

Also, it is necessary to assess the effects of traumatic experiences, sin, failures, disappointments, etc., since an entire life may be influenced by one significant event. For example, one young man whom I saw was fully grown at age 15 but found it necessary to have a home-bound teacher since he could not leave his home to go to school. The genesis of his problem was a tragic event at age 6 in which his father and brother were killed and his mother was injured. During the following year, he lost 4 other significant relatives who were both emotionally and geographically close. The emotional damage sustained during that period of time had rendered him helpless in facing the normal activities involved in growing up. At the time he saw me, he was too fearful to let go of the identity based on trauma in exchange for an identity based on the joy and peace of his new life in Christ.

All of that which has gone into our lives, both good and bad, serves to constitute the identity out of which we live. Since this identity is not based on who we are in Christ, it is based on time/space relationships which are always subject to change without notice. Though the identity might work well in a particular set of circumstances or culture, a radical change in any of these can result in a loss of identity or a decreased effectiveness in relating to the people and/or institutions with which we must deal.

One young man had his entire life wrapped up in becoming a physician. However, his test scores were too low to be admitted to medical school which destroyed his identity; all of his eggs were in one basket! As a result, he broke with reality and was on extremely heavy medication for a mental problem, when all he was facing was a total loss of identity. Though he was a believer, he was not living out of his identity in Christ but out of a human or fleshly identity. His new and true identity in Christ had nothing to do with his chosen profession, but he had made his goal of becoming a physician his total identity. When he was able to understand this and exchange the false identity for the true, he was freed from his psychotic condition and is presently living a fulfilling life in another profession. It will be helpful to read pp. 20-23 in *Handbook to Happiness* to expand your understanding of this vital topic of identity.

Once the old identity is thoroughly understood and embraced or owned, it is possible to release it in the power of the Holy Spirit in exchange for an identity that will never change for time or eternity. Though we have a new identity from our rebirth, we may not understand or appropriate it by faith during our entire sojourn on planet Earth. Even though many of the psychological conflicts with which we deal may have been thrust upon us from conception on through our developmental years, the fact that those which are non-organic remain after we are regenerated is a spiritual problem, though often fraught with many psychological symptoms. Let us now graphically portray some common conflicts in the personality or soul and contrast these with that which is true of the believer in the spirit.

II. THE DIAGNOSIS

The following study of the *Wheel and Line* is self-explanatory when used in conjunction with the scriptures; however, before attempting to present the answer to anyone else, it will be found helpful to digest Chapter 3 of *Counseling with the Mind of Christ*, A Simplified Model of Man. Also, it will be helpful to refer to *Gems and Jargon* for definitions of terms which are used in each of the books. It is not unusual for scriptural terms such as sin, flesh, old man, etc., to be used interchangeably or in an overlapping fashion in much teaching and writing. Though the Wheel Diagrams depict a model of man, the model contained in *Counseling with the Mind of Christ* (see Appendix C) will fortify the discipler with a more thorough understanding of the makeup and functioning of man. Also, Chapter 6 of *The Ins and Out of Rejection* provides a detailed description of the interaction of soul and spirit and a graphic representation of the terminology involved in Romans 6-8. Though it is too early to utilize this information with the one being discipled, being well grounded can be of immense value to the discipler in assessing both the psycho-social history of the individual, the spiritual condition, and stage of growth.

PRESENTING OR STUDYING THE WHEEL AND LINE

Introduction

During the past 20 years, thousands of believers in this and other countries have found victory or revival; and a number of unbelievers have trusted Christ as their Savior and Lord through an understanding given by the Holy Spirit of the scripture portrayed to them through these simple diagrams. Others have learned to share with those who are hurting, both lost and saved, how they may find comfort and victory in the Lord Jesus Christ. Reprints of this section may be obtained from the author for personal use or for training programs within the discipleship ministry of the church.

The diagrams contained herein are from *Handbook to Happiness*, (Chapter 2, revised edition); and it is assumed that you will have read that book (and, possibly, the *Wheel and Line* tract, available from the author) before embarking on this study. Having that background, a detailed study of this basic tool for communication should help to cement it in your mind; and I trust the Holy Spirit will apply its message to your heart and life, if that is not already the case.

If the Cross is presently a reality in your life, I trust the Holy Spirit will make of you an effective instrument in communicating that message, the foundation of revival, to those in your sphere of influence. Why not stop right here and pray again that the Holy Spirit will illuminate these truths from God's Holy Word to show you where you are in your spiritual journey and how He can provide the spiritual understanding upon which you may act that He will transform your life by renewing your mind? Good, now we are ready to begin!

Chapter 5 of *Counseling with the Mind of Christ* by the author will show you how you can share the message of the Cross using this material with another in a one-on-one setting; sometimes this is known as counseling, but it is really true discipleship as defined in Luke 14:27: "And whosoever doth not bear his cross, and come after me, cannot be my disciple."

The message herein contained is profoundly simple and simply profound! The most consistent criticism we have received over the past 22 years is that it is just too simplistic. My reply to that has been and is, "Amen"! If a Ph. D. were needed to understand it, most believers would be unable to avail themselves of needed help. It is the heart of the gospel which has never ceased to transform lives. The gospel for sinners is: Christ died for you; the gospel for saints is: you died, too! Both (which are really part of the same) are life transforming.

SETTING AND OBJECTIVES

1. Individual study of this presentation under the leadership of the Holy Spirit will make it necessary to interact with the material and foster assimilation of the truth which does not always happen through the reading of the book or tract or listening to a presentation by another.
2. Group study, discussion, and practice in communicating the believer's identity in Christ, the true revival message, to one another to become proficient in leading another believer to the Cross.
3. Church-wide training in discipleship by churches which are committed to meet the deepest needs of their members, many of whom are presently referred outside the church for answers.

Many have found the use of these diagrams to be very effective in sharing the gospel with the lost, not only in this culture but also in parts of the world where evangelism is very difficult. There are a number of churches where the members are routinely taught to share the *Wheel and Line* with the lost and with the saved. As you study it for yourself, keep in mind that it has proven transferable; and believers just like yourself have been greatly used of God in the lives of hurting people because they had a simple tool to communicate the depths of the gospel of our Lord and Savior, Jesus Christ, who alone is worthy to receive the glory.

OUTLINE

The material has been divided into seven sections:

A. Identity: A Crucial Construct
B. Adam's Identity before the Fall
C. Adam's Identity, or Man in Adam
D. The Self-Centered Believer, or the Fleshly Identity
E. The Foundation for the Exchanged Life
F. The Christ-Centered Believer, or Man in Christ
G. Prayers of Appropriation

A. IDENTITY: A CRUCIAL CONSTRUCT

Since the search for identity underlies much of the conscious or unconscious motivation for behavior, it will pay rich dividends to come to grips with this vital issue and put it on the table for study and discussion. Though each of us lives out of an identity, few of us ever identify that identity! Each person who is born of the Spirit is a new creation (2 Cor. 5:17) and, therefore, has a new identity. Many believers have little appreciation for the effect this new identity is to have in their lives. They marshal all of their resources to live for God for much or all of their sojourn on planet Earth. Since we were created in Christ Jesus unto good works (Eph. 2:10), we should serve; but since we are in Christ, our service should be out of our resources and identity in Him.

Since identity is such a crucial construct, it is vital that we see how important it is to make the transition from the Adamic and/or fleshly identity, to the identity that God desires for His children—that of being conformed to the image of the Lord Jesus Christ (Romans 12:1,2).

Jesus brought up the question of identity in Matthew 16:13-16 when He asked His disciples two questions: First, who others said that He was and, second, who they (the disciples) said that He was. You might ask yourself these same two questions: "Who have others said that you are?" and, "Who do you say that you are?" Questions to clarify them follow:

[] What have others said about you?

[] How did they treat you?

[] Do you agree with their evaluation, or are you still trying to prove them wrong? In what ways?

[] Are you still trying to build an identity and be somebody at work, in the home or at church? If so, how are you doing this?

[] Are you trying to prove something to someone? If so, what and to whom?

Given enough time and effort, you may build an identity of which you are justifiably proud! But, pride is nothing to brag about, either–at least before God! The real question to consider is, "Who does God say that you are?" Do you know? Do you care?

If you know and care, are you living out of it; or, are you trying to build a Christian identity based on what you do *for* Him? Explain:

The bottom line is, "Are you *doing* in order to *be*?" or, "Are you *being* in order to *do*? The first is of the law; the second is of grace. Are you *working* toward an identity, or are you *receiving* by faith your true identity in Christ? In the first, we work to build a life; and in the second, we lose our life that He might reveal His life in us (Gal. 1:16).

In order to understand ourselves and others and to make sense out of some of the things which have happened to us, it is necessary to have a model which encompasses both the psychological and spiritual dimensions of man. Also, it is crucial that we understand our nature and the strategic role it plays in our fundamental identity. The models which follow will aid us in getting perspective on our makeup and why identity plays such a key role in our behavior.

B. ADAM'S IDENTITY BEFORE THE FALL

We need first to consider Adam because it all began there. Adam was created as a spiritual being having a soul (personality) and living in a body. He enjoyed a perfect balance between spirit, soul, and body as depicted in Diagram 1; the arcs show the interaction between the three constituent parts. He related to God through an innocent spirit and, thus, found his total identity through his relationship with God. He was spiritually complete even before God presented Eve to him.

Diagram 1

Adam is depicted as a three part being, a tri-unity, sometimes known as the trichotomous view of man. With the body, through the senses, he could relate to his surroundings; and with the soul he could relate to others. You will note that Adam, prior to the Fall, had not yet become *flesh* in the sense of Gen. 6:3 (a condition where his whole being was under the control of a sin nature which he was yet to have); therefore, he had no internal conflict since he had an innocent spirit and was walking in total dependence upon God. Since his entire being was yielded to God, there is no center depicted in his life.

I Thessalonians 5:23 and Hebrews 4:12 are the prime proof texts that man's soul differs from his spirit. Though many other passages allude to the spirit, none is as succinct as these two. Though many dismiss the dichotomy/trichotomy issue of little consequence, a thoughtful study of this Spiritual Clinic can provide the reader with some food for thought. In the author's opinion, it is the spirit of man that makes him intrinsically different from the animal kingdom.

The body contains all that is included in the personal makeup, including the brain which contains the soul (my opinion), and the soul which contains the spirit. (Three concentric circles would provide a more adequate portrayal of our triune makeup, but it is more difficult to handle in explaining some of the constructs with which we have to deal in this study. See APPENDIX C.)

Prior to the Fall, Adam had an innocent spirit; and since he was walking in perfect union with God, he had no internal or external conflicts. His environment was not hostile, and he lived in perfect accord with his wife. (Believe it or not!)

Though he had a perfect identity, he had the choice to obey or disobey God. He had only one prohibition; and that was, "But of the tree of the knowledge of good and evil, thou shalt not eat of it: for in the day that thou eatest thereof thou shalt surely die" (Gen.2:17). This perfect identity was lost through Eve's deception by Satan and Adam's deliberate transgression. As a result, Adam became the recipient of *unrighteousness* by works; in other words, he sinned to become unrighteous! It was by his own doing, or works, that he became sinful or unrighteous. (Many believers are, likewise, deceived by the enemy of souls and are yet trying to establish *righteousness* by works, which is self-righteousness. As Galatians 3:3 puts it: "Are ye so foolish? having begun in the Spirit, are ye now made perfect by the flesh? " Though it is the flip side, it is still our own works upon which we are depending to gain favor with God, so long as we are living out of a fleshly identity.)

C. ADAM'S IDENTITY, OR MAN IN ADAM

Since Adam disobeyed God's explicit command which carried with it the death penalty, we must ask the question: "What kind of death took place?" It is obvious that it was not a physical death for the events of his life after this time are carefully chronicled in the ensuing chapters. Also, it is clear that his (her) soul or personality continued to function, albeit under a different source of power. After the Fall, however, they were unable spiritually to relate to God.

We might say that they had a type of reverse spiritual birth since they (and we) became children of the devil or alive to Satan. Through transgression Adam and Eve died out of God's family and were made part of (born into) Satan's family (John 8:44, 1 Jn. 3:10). Though it is not specifically stated in scripture, this had to signal the advent of the *old man* or unregenerate spirit of Romans 6:6. This spirit is separated from God and is in a state of continuous rebellion against Him. We are all born with such a spirit.

Diagram #2 represents Adam after the Fall and each of us as we are born into this life. The soul, or personality, consists of the functions of the mind, emotions and will. The *soul* might be called our self-consciousness or the means through which we relate to others. It is our psychological make-up.

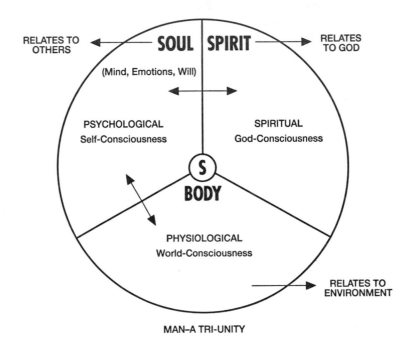

MAN–A TRI-UNITY

Diagram 2

The spirit is our capacity for God-consciousness or that aspect of our makeup by which we were intended to relate to God. The diagram represents Adam, where the spirit is dead to God and alive to Satan. (Obviously, the God-Consciousness or relating to God is not functioning so long as the spirit is unregenerate.) As a result, we are children of the devil (1 Jn. 3:10). Since we are alive to Satan, our life is part of Satan's family and nature, raging in disobedience, passions and wrath against ourself and others, being slaves to sin. Such is the result of our 'in Adam' identity!

At physical birth God's spirit-life is not in us. We were created as spiritual beings; but Adam, in disobeying God, died out of God's family (Gen. 2:17, Rom. 6:23), and we in him: "For as in Adam all die" (1 Cor. 15:22). As descendants of Adam, we are born into this world already spiritually dead to God and are part of Adam's nature. As those who are of Satan's family, we are very much alive to him. This being the case, we are only doing what comes naturally when we commit sins (Rom.3:23). Even though we may live very good lives, humanly speaking, we are separated from God unless and until we are born into His family by a spiritual rebirth.

As we have seen previously, the soul or personality has three different functions: the mind, emotions, and will. The mind is the seat of intelligence, reason, and memory; it might be called our *thinker*. The emotions (or *feelers*) enable us to relate in a feeling way to those around us and to express such things as love and anger, elation and despair.

The will is the decider between the mind and emotions or between truth and error, and we might term it our *chooser*. Often the mind and emotions are in conflict with one another. Whether we react more strongly intellectually or emotionally depends on how our *will* responds and whether we have been programmed to act out of our thought processes or out of our feelings.

There is a continuous interaction between the soul and spirit and the soul and body as shown through the interconnecting arrows. Though we show lines of demarcation, we are not so neatly compartmentalized that we can have a problem in one area without affecting another. If we get hurt physically, we might react in pain, anger, or bitterness. If we have emotional conflict, there can be resulting physical or bodily involvement. Too, physical problems, such as glandular dysfunction or brain tumor, can have a psychological impact.

Before salvation, the spirit (or old man) of the unbeliever holds the soul captive to sin; as a result, we are slaves to sin. Contrary or damaged emotions may make it difficult to walk in accord with the truth known to the mind. As conflicts and circumstances become difficult, the soul, acting independently of God's spirit, may be unable to cope; and a variety of mental/emotional and physical symptoms may arise.

The 'S' in the diagram stands for that which is the central focus or driving force in our lives.

[] What drives you or is your highest ambition?
Or, what gives you meaning?

Before Christ came into our lives, we all had to live in our own resources. The S may represent a multitude of things or people; but back of that, *we* are deciding *what* or *who* will maintain this controlling position. Ultimately, the S stands for Self which we will be using synonymously with flesh. It should be noted that Self in this sense does not refer to the personality as is inferred by some. When Adam sinned, he became flesh (Gen. 6:3); and when we are born, we are "in the flesh" (Rom. 8:8). Absent the new birth, the only other possibility besides *self* for the central position in the life is Satan; in either event, the S fits! (And, sometimes, *has* fits!)

D. THE SELF-CENTERED BELIEVER, OR THE FLESHLY IDENTITY

Though *Self* remains in the center as in Diagram 2, the following model represents a far different situation. Diagram 3 illustrates that which results in a *condition* of the soul in the believer but is a *permanent position* with the lost person; in other words, the believer has a choice but the lost person does not–his soul is under the control of the old man or sin nature. For diagrammatic purposes, the *condition* is represented by the *S* at the center of the life; however, it is more accurate to say that *Self* or *Flesh* (KJV) is a condition of the soul or personality. This condition is in force when the believer has yielded to indwelling sin (Rom.6:13), intentionally or unintentionally. *Flesh* or *Self* is not a fourth part of the human being. It is this condition, *Flesh* or *Self,* from which sins emanate in the life of the believer as indicated in Galatians 5:16,19-21–not from the old nature as is so generally taught. The *effects* in the Soul or Personality are depicted in Diagram 4.

Diagram 3

The C in the lower part of the spirit portion of the circle represents Christ in the life, or a person indwelt by the Holy Spirit, a Christian. This person has been born again (or born from above) in his spirit by the Holy Spirit (John 3:3). The regenerate spirit may now be called the new man of Colossians 3:9,10, which is sometimes referred to as the new nature. *The identity of the believer is based on the family in which he is or, better, on the Person* in Whom *he is.* As we have shown previously, prior to regeneration a person is in Adam (This will be explained in greater detail in the *Line Diagram* which follows).

[] Do you consider yourself to be a Christian?

[] State in your own words how you believe a person becomes a Christian.

In Diagram 3, the word,

1. *Salvation,* is restricted to the spiritual birth which results in our being part of God's family, though it could encompass the totality of redemption. Only through spiritual rebirth can we leave the life of Adam and be born into the life of Christ, which is eternal life. To be born spiritually, we must recognize or confess that we are in the wrong life, or born as sinners, with the unavoidable result that we have committed sins (Rom. 3:23). Then, we must repent of our sins and trust Christ as our Savior and Lord, if we are to know Him in the forgiveness of our sins and to receive His life (Rom. 10:9,10,13).

In being born spiritually, those who receive the Spirit-life of Christ into their spirit by faith (John 1:12), become one spirit with Him (1 Cor. 6:17).

[] Describe the circumstances that led to your
salvation experience or justification:

2. If the believer is to have victory over sin and
experience the peace of God in his life, he must have
assurance of his salvation. Assurance must be based on
the absolutes of God's inerrant Word or it will be
fleeting at best.

Many who know (with their minds) that they have
personally trusted the Lord Jesus Christ still lack
genuine assurance because they have never *felt* saved.
Because of emotional conflicts, many of which stem
from childhood rejection, a person's feelings (or
emotions) may seldom be in harmony with the
facts–including the truths delineated in the Bible and
those existing in the physical world. The way we feel
things to be is likely to differ from how they really are
until Christ becomes central in our lives and heals the
damaged emotions.

It is possible for a person to lack adequate
scriptural foundation on which to base assurance of
salvation and actually to doubt his salvation. In this
case, impartation of truth from the Word can clear up
doubts, as the believer acts in faith on that which he
needs to understand.

[] Have you experienced difficulty with
Assurance? If so, list some ways it has been
manifested in your life and how it has affected you.

3. *Security.*

[] Have you ever doubted the security of your relationship with God? Why?

We see that the believer, old or new, must know that he enters into a secure, eternal, spiritual relationship with God through the Lord Jesus Christ (John 5:24, I John 5:11-13, Romans 8:16, Heb. 13:5) and that he can rely upon and enjoy that relationship without fear of interruption.

Though many believers know that they have accepted Christ, few understand and experience the truth that they are accepted *in Him.* Most have been forced to earn acceptance on a human basis and feel they also must earn God's

4. *Acceptance*–Even though they have already been accepted entirely through their Christ-Life (Eph. 1:6) they may never appropriate it by faith. Every believer is accepted, but many never accept, by faith, their acceptance, or righteousness (2 Cor. 5:21) in Christ.
To illustrate the importance of acceptance, consider the following questions:

[] On what basis does God accept Christ?

[] How much does God accept Christ?

[] Is there anything that Christ could do to lose that relationship?

[] Is your relationship with God through Christ (Col. 3:3)?

[] How much then does God accept you in Christ (Phil. 1:6, John 10:28,29, John 6:37-40)?

5. Few, too, are those who make *Total Commitment* or total surrender of their lives to the Lord Jesus Christ. Though a person can not be saved if he makes a conscious choice not to yield to the lordship of Christ, there are those who yield to all they know of Christ at salvation but discover later that they have not yielded all to Him. This is an irrevocable decision which indicates our willingness to have our Father do anything He desires in us, with us, to us, or through us. We give up our right to independence. It is an act of the will which may or may not be accompanied by immediate discernible changes, intrapersonally or interpersonally. Since our Father has our permission to 'work on our case', He may proceed slowly or rapidly depending upon our continued yieldedness to the teaching and work of the Holy Spirit in our lives.

It is important to note here that total surrender and the Christ-centered life are not necessarily synonymous, though they could and should be! In fact, the *S* at the center of the life is the plight of many believers until they finally find Christ as their Life in Glory! By then, however, they have forfeited the opportunity of experiencing increasing conformity to the image of Christ in our walk here on Earth. This is a travesty on the gospel which should never be.

Before you continue, here are some questions that you will do well to answer about your relationship with God.

[] How would you describe your relationship with God?

[] How do you define total commitment to Christ?

[] Have you ever made a total surrender to Christ, giving up all of your rights to yourself and to control your life? If so, when?

[] Is Christ the center of your life, or are you allowing something or someone else to occupy this central position?

[] If Christ is the center of your life, how and when did the Holy Spirit make the Cross a reality in your experience?

Only if you have made a total surrender to Christ will your life begin to be conformed to the image of Christ (Rom. 8:29). Total surrender can very well signal the beginning of the process of brokenness which will eventuate in your coming to know Christ as your life. If you have never made such a total surrender, would you be willing to pray a prayer such as, "Lord, break me."? Or, "Lord, I now yield my life and everything and everyone related to it to you to be disposed of as you see fit; I surrender to you as Lord of my life." If you have not made an absolute surrender to God, the only remaining option is that you are yet fighting God; it is most difficult to have peace with God while, at the same time, actively or passively fighting Him!

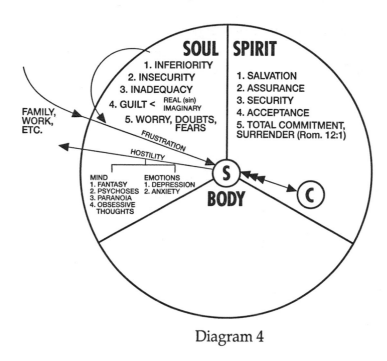

Diagram 4

The *S* at the center of the wheel in Diagram 4 represents the self-controlled life. The Bible calls it flesh. Flesh can take differing avenues, depending upon the individual, to get its needs met by something or someone, in either a negative or a positive way. When a person is dominated by the self-life, money, material things, success, fame, sex, power or any of countless other things can drive or motivate him. An overly simplified definition of the flesh is a person's attempt to live the Christ-life in his own strength, which is an obvious contradiction in terms.

When this is the Christian's condition, five common responses appear in the soul or the psychological makeup. Obviously, there are those who have the positive counterparts of these more negative personality traits. These individuals tend to have a

45

greater problem, because they think they do not have a problem! (See Part II, Chapter 5 of *The Ins and Out of Rejection*, The Perils of the Well-Adjusted) Do any of these characteristics describe your life?

1. *Inferiority* feelings–these generally result from our having been compared negatively with others or making such invidious comparisons ourselves. Thus, we may interpret our life and circumstances out of our feelings which has an effect on our *being* as well as our *doing*.

[] Do you feel inferior to others when, deep down, you know that you are not? Explain.

2. *Insecurity*–that which relates primarily to our relationship with others.

[] Do you question your position of trust and assurance with others?

[] Is jealousy a problem with which you struggle?

[] Do you live with a constant, low-level fear?

3. *Inadequacy*–that which relates primarily to performance.

[] Do you question your ability to discharge responsibilities?

4. *Guilt*– Real guilt is caused by sins of commission or omission. The only answer is the Blood of the Lord Jesus Christ appropriated through faith by confession and repentance.

[] Is there any sin in your life with which you have not dealt in this way? Ask the Holy Spirit to reveal any unconfessed sin and confess and forsake (repent) it right now.

False or imaginary guilt can have its basis in the lack of self-forgiveness after having received God's forgiveness. It can also be caused by being told or being treated as though we were not wanted, making us feel guilty for being in the world.

Imaginary guilt can be as destructive as real guilt, but its basis may be unknown. There may, therefore, be endless confession with no lessening of the guilt feeling.

False guilt and accusations by the enemy are fertile ground for growing defeat in the life of a believer. When coupled with damaged emotions, it all adds up to a pack of lies which are in constant conflict with truth that may be known in the mind.

[] Are you plagued with guilt feelings for which you have found no resolution? If so, can you identify what you feel guilty about?

[] Could it be that you still feel guilty or hold yourself guilty over sin which you have scripturally confessed and forsaken?

5. *Worries, doubts, and fears*–We might include all of these under the umbrella of negative faith or unbelief. We allow the pressures of life–past, present and future–to dominate our thinking, and we find ourselves in a state of discouragement and defeat.

[] In your life, what are the significant events to which such thinking is attached?

The psychological deficiencies, along with real and imagined guilt and the pressures of life combine to produce varying degrees of frustration in the self-controlled life (represented by the inwardly directed line in the soul). This frustration must be dealt with. Some choose to dump it on others in the form of blows–physical or verbal. Others are more afraid of retaliation and suppress their hostility as best they can. Others suppress anger and frustration because they blame themselves for every problem and annoyance they encounter and feel that they deserve what they get; or, they may fear further rejection.

When hostility and frustration are suppressed, for whatever reason, they will have an impact in the mind or emotions or both. Internalized hostility or anger often results in depression and/or anxiety in the emotions. Some persons can use their minds to implement various distortions or denial of reality, as listed in the diagram. (Some of these breaks with reality may be organic in origin such as with the chronic schizophrenic; the organic, as opposed to functional, problem is beyond the scope of this study since it is a medical issue.) The flight from reality, or running away in their heads, enables them to escape the necessity of dealing with the real problem, self-centeredness or flesh. Most people who are into denial do not have access to the knowledge that self-centeredness is the basic problem; often, this is reinforced by conventional therapy which addresses the symptoms rather than the problem.

[] Have you experienced any of these problems in your life? Explain.

[] How have you tried to deal with them?

When the psychological conflict drags on without remedy, it commonly results in physical complaints, as illustrated in Diagram 5. The physical ailments, though real, actually are symptoms of a deeper problem—self-centeredness or flesh. So are the psychological symptoms depicted in the *soul* area from which the physical symptoms emanate. Though they may have had their genesis in childhood trauma, the fact that they remain as a force in the life after rebirth is indicative that the liberating power of the Holy Spirit has not been effected in the personality in a manner which resolves them.

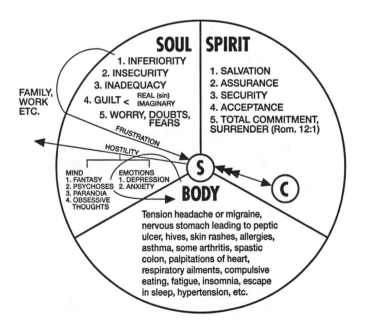

Diagram 5

Can you see that, if you are approaching life with these attitudes about yourself and in your own resources, under stress your self-life (flesh) will not be able to cope? Do you see that the result will be hostility or anger acted outward toward others or inward toward yourself?

As we have seen, emotional responses to internal stress can result in anxiety and depression. As the mind attempts to handle stress, some choose to escape through such things as alcohol, drugs, divorce, television, sex, work, or even Christian service (which may be more for us than for the Lord).

[] Have you been experiencing any physical symptoms that could be caused by stress? If so, what are they?

[] Can you see that your symptoms may be the result of your self-life being unable to handle the pressures of life?

[] Do you understand the diagram and how we may react and deal with problems if we are self-centered? Do you think this is the kind of life that God has called you to? Is this the abundant life that God has promised to those who make a total commitment to Christ? If we are even reasonably honest, we must answer, "No".

[] Based on what you have seen so far, do you understand that your problem is not your circumstances or those people who have hurt you in the past or present, or your psychological conflict?

[] Do you see that, though your circumstances may be problematic, they reveal the real problem–that self resources are inadequate to handle the pressures of life? List some of the negative circumstances and/or relationships which are forcing you to assess your life in every area:

We must now see if you can determine what you have been doing to solve your problems. Remember; the self-life is what the Bible calls flesh.

[] In trying to resolve your problems in your own strength, have you asked God to help you?

[] Does Christ want to help the flesh? Read Gal. 5:17, and see if God would ever take sides with the flesh!

[] Have you asked God to strengthen you? How? When?

[] Does the Spirit want to strengthen the flesh? Read Galatians 3:3.

[] Have you asked God to lead, guide, direct, and control you?

[] Does the Spirit want to guide or control the flesh? Read Romans 8:6.

God may have honored such requests for guidance in the past because you prayed them sincerely, but now He desires to show you something better. God's intent is to allow you to experience an exchanged life. This exchange of your self-life for His Life is His solution for your problem.

When a person does make a total surrender to Christ, circumstances frequently degenerate into near chaos afterward. God honors our request for Him to take complete control of our lives. If He is to take control, we must lose control; and that is a process that seldom gives us joy! But if *we* remain in control, we are really *out* of control!

It is even more distressing when the circumstances or persons God uses to bring us to the end of control of our own lives are often not, in themselves, spiritual. They, sometimes, inflict undeserved suffering; but it is just such suffering that accomplishes God's purposes in our lives (1 Pet. 2:20-21; Phil. 1:23-30). At the time, the suffering or chastening seldom seems a cause for rejoicing, but it is the crucible that produces the holiness for which we long in our spirits (Phil. 3:10; Heb. 12:11).

God's purpose for the believer is to conform him to the image of Christ (Rom. 8:29), and that involves suffering (Phil.1:29,30, 3:10). Though it may not appear so at the time, these are part of the "all things" of Romans 8:28 which work together for our good.

III. SPIRITUAL SURGERY

E. THE FOUNDATION FOR THE EXCHANGED LIFE

In order to see how you can exchange the self-life or fleshly identity for the Christ-life, it is necessary for you to have a clear understanding of what the scripture teaches in this regard; it is usually studied under the heading of sanctification. There are a number of opinions on this vital doctrine, but our purpose here is to bring into focus the Cross and its vital work in the life of the believer. In thinking through a topic which receives too little attention in the ministry of the average church, it may prove helpful for you to answer the following questions:

[] What does the term, *eternal life*, mean to you?

[] When does eternal life begin?

[] *Whose* life is eternal?

[] If you said, "It is my life"; what is the source of that eternal life ?

[] What do we mean when we say that God is eternal?

[] Then, what is eternal life? (John 17:3, John 1: 1,2; 1 John 1:2, 5:20).

It becomes obvious that eternal life does not begin when we die or when we are saved, as so many of us have deduced; but we do enter into it at the point of our salvation. It is clear from scripture that he who has Christ has eternal life in Him (1 Jn 5:11).

The line in Diagram 6 symbolizes eternal life, a life without beginning or end. You can see that Jesus Christ came into the world (Jn 1:14), lived about 33 years, died on the cross, was buried, raised on the third day (1 Cor. 15:3,4) and ascended (Acts 1:9) and is today living the same life (Heb. 13:8). While in the body, He lived the same life that He had from eternity past; and it is the same life that He lives today at the right hand of the Father (Heb. 12:2) and in each born again believer (Col.1:27).

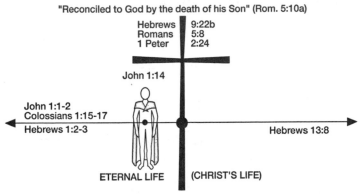

"Reconciled to God by the death of his Son" (Rom. 5:10a)

"So by the obedience of one shall many be made righteous" (Rom. 5:19b)

Diagram 6

At this point, there are a few questions that we must ask about the life of the Lord Jesus:

[] Why did Jesus Christ die? (Romans 5:8, 1 Pet. 2:24)

[] Do you understand that since Christ paid for your sins on the cross, that if you are in Him, God will never punish you for them?

[] Can you see that Christ as your life will never change?

Remember that Christ's life never changes; and, therefore, even though your soul (feeling, thinking, choosing) *may* change, and your body *will* change, your Life (Christ) will *never* change!

But when you entered this world, you were not born of an eternal life. You and I were born into another existence that is called "Life in Adam" as illustrated in Diagram 7. For a moment, let us set aside what we know about Adam and Eve and the Fall and consider what the word, *in*, means. First, we will consider the implications of being *in* Adam; and, then, we will study the results of being *in* Christ.

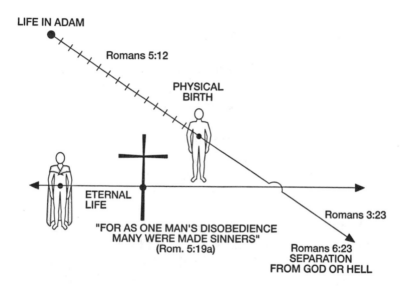

Diagram 7

Let the figure in the diagonal line represent you as you showed up on planet Earth and the hatch marks represent your parents, grandparents and their ancestors all the way back to Adam. Can you see that if your parents had died, or one of your ancestors had died without having children, that you would have shown up missing? Furthermore, if Adam and Eve had produced no children, we would have had very little to talk or write about! Can you see that your life proceeded from Adam in an unbroken life chain through each of your ancestors and that it is inescapable that your physical and spiritual lives were inherited from him?

If you see this, then, where were you when Adam was in the Garden of Eden? Do you see that you had to be in him because your life was *in him*? It is apparent, then, that each of us was identified with Adam in his sin and his subsequent death because of that sin.

The results of being in Adam are as follows:

We sinned (Rom. 5:12) and continue to sin (Rom. 3:23) such that ". . .the wages of sin is death; but the gift of God is eternal life through Jesus Christ our Lord" (Rom. 6:23).

We died (speaking of spiritual death, or separation from God). Adam's spirit died which means that he could no longer relate to God; being in him we died at the same time (1 Cor. 15:22). I have inferred that it was Adam's spirit which died since he was still functioning in his body and soul (personality or psychological makeup) after a type of death took place. God said he would die in the day that he sinned (Gen. 2:17); therefore, we conclude that he died immediately even though he continued to live. It seems conclusive that it had to be a spiritual death with extensive psychological and even physical ramifications; though the body didn't die immediately, the death sentence was upon it from that moment forward.

We were condemned (Rom. 3:10-12; Rom. 5:16b-18; Rom. 6:23). Our future wages in Adam is death in Hell (solitary, eternal separation from God).

Although you were condemned in Adam, God made provision for your salvation. Diagram 8 shows how we are transferred from the kingdom of darkness to the kingdom of light in salvation and how the exchanged life is part and parcel of our new birth. The curved line from the Adam-life to the Christ-life depicts being removed from the life of Adam and placed into the Life of Christ (Col. 1:13, 1 Cor. 1:30, John 1:12,13, Rom. 10:13). All of us who have been born of the Spirit have been baptized into Christ or placed into His Life (Rom. 6:3).

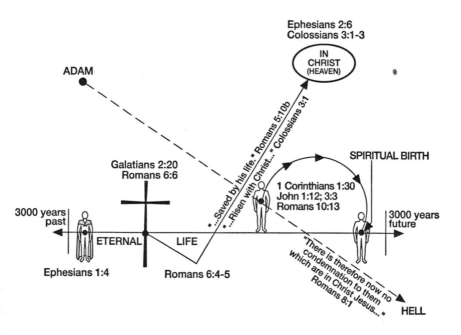

Diagram 8

When we are born or placed into Christ's life, a death and a birth takes place simultaneously: We die out of Adam's life by co-crucifixion (Rom. 6:3-11; Gal. 2:20), and we are born into Christ's life (Rom. 6:4-6; Col. 3:1-4) by co-resurrection. At the beginning of this study, we asked the question, "When Adam died as the scriptures assert, what died?". We concluded that it was, of necessity, a spiritual death. Now, we come to a similar juncture where a death is said to have taken place: "Knowing this, that our old man is crucified with him. . ." (Rom. 6:6); "For he that is dead is freed from sin." (Rom. 6:7); "I am crucified with Christ. . ." (Gal. 2:20). While there are those who would make this a judicial or positional death, the Word states unequivocally that we died! It is a past completed fact.

Since we know we were crucified with Christ, we are commanded to count it to be so (Rom. 6:11)–not to debate as to whether a death took place! Not only have we died, but we have also been made alive in resurrection life as stated in Rom. 6:4,5 and other places. Again, it had to be a spiritual death–the death of the old man or unregenerate spirit–just as we had a spiritual birth and now have a regenerate spirit or new man (Col. 3:10). Since we are now the new man, God can and does declare us righteous (2 Cor. 5:21)! Only the regenerate spirit indwelt by the Holy Spirit could qualify for that description. It is easy to see, therefore, why we believe that the scriptures make plain that man has a spirit–not just a body and soul (1 Thes. 5:23; Heb. 4:12).

Returning to the theme of identity, it is now obvious that our true identity is that of the *new man*, not that of the *old man*. Our identity derives from the family in which we find ourselves; and we died out of the old family (Adam's) and have been born into a new one (God's). *Not only do we get a new future, but we also get a new past*! Hallelujah! Do you know of anyone who could not use a new past? On a sign in front of a church once I saw this sign, "A sinner has no future, and a Christian has no past!" Psychologists and psychiatrists spend extraordinary amounts of time dealing with past events in a person's life and the impact of those antecedent events on the person's intrapersonal and interpersonal functioning. However, they are powerless to do anything about a person's past other than to understand and deal with the results of it in present experience. The Holy Spirit is under no such limitations of time; when we enter into a new life, it has a new future and a new past as well as a victorious present! He is fully capable of healing us from emotional disturbances caused by childhood trauma; His analysis is thorough and perfect, and His resources for transforming our lives are inexhaustible. A Spirit-given understanding of this new identity in Christ results in living out of a new life–His life, resurrection life!

So, as believers, we are not to live out of a patched up identity based on the forgiveness of sins alone; but we are to live out of our new identity, the new man. This new life is in resurrection power with victory by faith over the world, the flesh and the devil (I Jn. 4:4), because faith is the victory (1 John 5:4,5). Based on our co-death and co-resurrection with Christ, we can by faith exchange the self-life with its defeat for the Christ-Life with its victory.

Out of which identity are you living? Is it who *others* say you are? Is it who *you* say you are? Or, is it who *God* says you are? He ascribes to you as a believer a perfect and powerful identity which will not change for time nor eternity. Any other identity out of which you may be living is always subject to change without notice!

Have you counted the cost? Are you willing to lose your life? It is a divine paradox that we must fail in order to succeed; we must die in order to live. "Then said Jesus unto his disciples, If any man will come after me, let him deny himself, and take up his cross, and follow me. For whosoever will save his life shall lose it: and whosoever will lose his life for my sake shall find it." (Matthew 16:24,25) "Verily, verily, I say unto you, Except a corn of wheat fall into the ground and die, it abideth alone: but if it die, it bringeth forth much fruit. He that loveth his life shall lose it; and he that hateth his life in this world shall keep it unto life eternal." (John 12:24,25)

Let's review some of the principles we have been considering:

[] After Christ was crucified what happened to Him?

[] As a result, what happened to you (in spirit)? (Rom. 6:4,5)

[] After Christ rose from the dead, what happened to Him?

[] As a result, what happened to you (in spirit)? (Eph. 2:6)

[] Then, where are you today?

[] If you are placed into Christ now, then where were you (in spirit) when Christ was on the Cross? What happened to you there? (Rom. 6:6; Gal. 2:20; Rom. 5:16b) In summary, we were placed into Christ's death, and raised up with Him, and are seated with Him in the heavenly places in Christ Jesus. (Eph. 2:6)

[] Do you understand that, if you have exchanged your life in Adam for eternal life, your life is in Christ, or a Christ-life? And, only He can live His life.

[] Do you realize that your present life is *in Christ* (Phil.1:21); your past is *in Christ* (Eph. 1:4); and your future is *in Christ* (John 11:25,26)?

[] Do you recognize that you are dead to sin and alive to God if you have been born into His life (Rom. 6:11)?

Why do you suppose that God arranged for your death? It was so you could lose your life and exchange it for His. Can you see that God not only dealt with your sins but the *source* of your sins–the spirit that was dead to God and alive to Satan–or the old man (Rom. 6:6). Because the old man has been crucified with Christ (Rom. 6:6) and put off (Col. 3:9,10) and the new man has been put on, you can now, in obedience to God's Word, count yourself to be dead to sin and alive unto God in Christ Jesus (Rom. 6:11). As you do, the Holy Spirit will witness to truth and make real in your experience that it is no longer you who lives but Christ that lives in you (Gal. 2:20). This presumes that you have seen the utter futility of living out of the fleshly identity and are prepared for God's remedy for it.

By understanding the truth represented by these diagrams, has the Holy Spirit convicted you of the sin of rebellion or idolatry by living with *Self* at the center of the life instead of Christ? If so, victory is merely a prayer away; and you can know the abundant life as represented in the following diagram. Just as it is necessary for the Holy Spirit to convict us of sin before we are ready to be born again or regenerated, it is, likewise, necessary that we are convicted of the flesh and have been broken of self-sufficiency or self-dependency if we are to be prepared for Him to reveal to us our new life in Christ. Once you have studied this diagram and the corresponding scriptures, some suggested prayers follow that you might appropriate by faith all that Christ is for all that you need.

F. THE CHRIST-CENTERED BELIEVER OR MAN IN CHRIST

Diagram 9

Diagram 9 shows the results of the exchanged life, where Christ is in His proper place at the center. Not only is He the center; He is also the circumference! He is in us (Col. 1:27), but we are also in Him (1 Cor. 1:30). The book, *In Christ Jesus*, by A. T. Pierson does a masterful job of depicting this truth.

The self-life is dealt with by our reckoning, or counting, upon our co-death and co-resurrection with Christ. To put it another way, we have denied ourself and taken up the Cross and lost our life in order to save it. (Luke 9:23; John 12:24,25) (We are not actually dying at this point; we are merely counting by faith on the death we died when we were saved, but we may not have been aware of it.) Typically, the new believer is adequately instructed that he must be born (John 3:3); but he is not told that he died. As a result, he starts off, or soon begins, trying to live the Christian life in his own strength. Usually, he even thinks he has two lives at the same time–Adam's life and Christ's life. In order to have Adam's life we would have to be *in Adam*, but scripture clearly teaches that the believer is *in Christ*. The believer's problem, therefore, is not the Adam-life but, rather, the Flesh in conflict with the Spirit which is clearly defined in Galatians 5:17 and aptly described in Romans 7.

God's design is for you to experience rest in your soul (Heb. 4:9,10). As we walk in His life, our soul begins to be transformed (Rom. 12:2), and we are in the process of being conformed to His image (Rom. 8:29).

The following scriptures are some examples of God's intention:

1. That we might have the mind of Christ (Phil. 2:5) If Christ made Himself of no reputation, can we not expect to walk in humility without feeling inferior?

2. That we might do all things through the strength given by Christ (Phil. 4:13). If we have Christ's perfect strength, how can we be inadequate?

3. That we might have all of our needs supplied by Christ Jesus (Phil. 4:19). If our needs are being supplied, will we have cause for worry, doubts and fears?

4. That we might have the peace that surpasses understanding guarding our hearts and minds through Christ Jesus (Phil. 4:6,7). If we experience His peace, how can feelings of insecurity continue to be a way of life?

5. That we might have fullness of joy (John 15:11). If we bear much fruit (John 15:8), we have joy while the blood of Christ removes guilt for sins (I John 1:7). A fruitful life removes any reason to feel guilty.

As the soul is transformed by the Holy Spirit through the renewing of the mind, the body will begin losing some of the symptoms produced by the anxiety of trying to live the Christian life which only Christ can live. It, then, becomes possible for us to respond in the Spirit, instead of reacting after the flesh, to those circumstances and people whom God brings or allows to be part of our lives *and* to those things in our past which have governed our lives in many respects–even after we are born from above.

G. PRAYERS OF APPROPRIATION OR MAKING THE EXCHANGE

In order to know Christ as your life, it is necessary to go through the total relinquishing of your life to Jesus Christ as Lord of all. This is a radical act of the will, despite the tug of emotions and relationships to the contrary. To enter into the blessings of your identification with Christ you must be willing to let Him do anything He desires with you, your family, future, job, money, marriage, health, goals, relationships, etc.

Will you relinquish control and abandon yourself to Him, admitting that, in and of yourself, you are an absolute failure and give up your rights to your life and fleshly behavior patterns–the bad and the good? Has the Holy Spirit convicted you of the rottenness of the Flesh and all that emanates from it? Are you truly sick of yourself and ready to quit shifting the blame such that others must change for you to be different? Or, that another person must change first? Have you dealt with all known sin in your life by confession and repentance?

If you are ready to do business with God, the following time-line might help you to assess where you are in your earthly sojourn. A more detailed description of the Paths to the Cross may be found beginning at page 93 of *Handbook to Happiness* or on page 154 of *The Ins and Out of Rejection*.

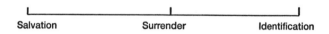

| Salvation | Surrender | Identification |

Diagram 10

It may be that you have come to a new understanding of Jesus' work on the Cross for you and have found that you have never been born of the Spirit. In that event, it would be appropriate for you to bow you head right now and trust Christ as your Savior and Lord. You might pray a prayer such as the following:

SALVATION PRAYER

"Heavenly Father, I have seen that I am a sinner still in the life of Adam and that I have committed sins. I believe you sent your only Son, the Lord Jesus Christ, to die in my place for my sins. I also believe He rose again and now lives, and right now I receive Him into my spirit as my Savior. I surrender all that I am, all that I have and all I ever shall be to you to be Lord of my life. I turn from my sins and my selfish ways to live my new life in Christ. Thank you for saving me from my sins and from myself for Jesus' sake. Amen."

If you have prayed the 'Salvation Prayer' after having been prepared by the Holy Spirit, you have been born again, for God says He gives to all who believe in Christ and call upon his name the privilege of becoming his children (John 1:12, Rom. 10:13).

As a result of this study, you may have come to grips with the fact that you have never made a total surrender (the next point on the time-line) of all that you have and are and ever will be to Jesus as Lord. You may even have surrendered in the past but never recognized your need or knew it possible to enter into the reality of your identification with Christ in death and resurrection. In either case, it won't hurt you to renew your surrender, and it can *certainly* help you to ". . . reckon yourselves to be dead indeed unto sin, but alive unto God through Jesus Christ our Lord" (Romans 6:11).

PRAYER OF TOTAL SURRENDER:

"Father, I can see that I have never totally relinquished my life to You for whatever purpose you brought me to Yourself; and, in so doing, I have denied your lordship in my life. Having counted the cost, I do hereby surrender my entire life to You without reservation—whether relationships, possessions, goals, health, reputation, wealth of whatever variety, emotional conflicts, fears, and everything that means anything. I confess the sin of living in my own strength which is really idolatry, pride and unbelief. It is my desire to live in total obedience to Your revealed Word and to that with which You impress me as Your perfect will for my life. Please bring to pass in my life that which will bring glory to You and grace and peace to me for Jesus' sake. Amen."

Whether you prayed to receive Christ just now or in the past, praying the "Selfer's Prayer" may help you to experience Christ's Life of victory and peace. Before this prayer can be effective, you must be truly sick of your self-life; you must be under conviction by the Holy Spirit of trying to live the Christian life in your own strength, and you must be ready to give up control and lose your life, even if none of the adverse circumstances change. If this is where you are right now, please pray the "Selfer's Prayer" and trust the Holy Spirit to make real Christ's life for your life and to fill you with His peace, power and joy.

THE SELFER'S PRAYER OR IDENTIFICATION WITH CHRIST

"Father, I admit that I'm a selfer, and have been struggling in my own resources to live the Christian life. I confess that my life is a failure and a mess. I come confessing my sin and rebellion against you, and I now give up my life and affirm with You my death with Christ. I also affirm that I have been raised with Christ and am seated in Him in the heavenly places. In accordance with your command, I deny myself and reckon myself to be dead to sin and alive to you. I give You complete control of myself and every thing or person I'm hanging onto to meet my needs. Do with me whatever you choose. I thank you for saving me from my sins and from my wicked self. From this moment on, I am trusting you to do what I can't do, quit what I can't quit, and, most of all, to be what I can't be! I now thank you that Christ is my life, my victory and my all. Thank you for filling me with your Spirit. Amen."

Victory is by faith initially and continually. We are saved from *sin* by grace through faith (Eph. 2:8,9), and we are saved from *ourselves* by grace through faith. However, victory *obtained* must result in victory *maintained* through taking up our Cross daily (Luke 9:23) and continually (2 Cor. 4:11). It is one thing to take that initial step of being filled with the Spirit (Eph. 5:18); but it is equally important that we walk in the Spirit (Gal. 5:16)–a repeated step. It is my prayer that God will use this message to meet you at your point of need and that you, in turn, might be used to His glory in sharing the message of victory and revival with believers and the message of salvation with the lost.

FOLLOW UP

Those who appropriate by faith the victory that ensues from an experiential understanding of identification with Christ will profit greatly by on-going discipleship in maintaining their walk in Christ. Those who do not have access to such fellowship will find a difficult path in trying to walk consistently in victory on their own. This is not to say that the Word and the Holy Spirit are insufficient, but God ordained the church as the institution which should provide the necessary fellowship with Him and with each other (I John 1:3). Blessed, indeed, is the believer who has access to one-on-one and group discipleship that he may not only be filled with the Spirit (Eph. 5:16) but also that he might be assisted in learning the walk in the Spirit (Galatians 5:16).

Such *koinonia* or fellowship groups are called support groups in the world system; of course, too many churches have picked up on that terminology and many new believers think that 12 step programs invented the idea! The church had such groups almost 2000 years before cell groups and support groups were even conceived; in fact, the church *was* and *is* such a group when it is functioning as an organism instead of an organization!

There are many good materials available to assist in the corporate discipleship process. However, most do not inculcate the centrality of the Cross in the sense we have been using it in this book. Once a believer understands who he is in Christ, *Master Life*, published by Broadman can be used to good advantage.

We have found that the little booklet by Norman B. Harrison, *New Testament Living*, is excellent for group study and discussion. It contains 13 lessons on the teaching of the Cross throughout the New Testament and has questions at the end of the book on each lesson.

It is my conviction that a believer who appropriates by faith the blessing to be obtained through our union with Christ in death and resurrection should be in a *koinonia* group for 6 months to one year which is led by a mature believer. In addition, there should be one-on-one discipleship weekly for a year, if at all possible. I realize that this is a major time commitment on the part of a discipler, and it can only be done if the church is truly functioning as the body of Christ. Some have found the book by Dr. Harold Burchett, *"Spiritual Life Studies, A Manual for Personal Edification*, to be excellent as a guide for individual discipleship.

Along with the discipline of formal discipleship, there must be the continued study of the Word, particularly in Paul's letters. Too, the reading of books such as are listed in APPENDIX A can be of invaluable assistance in understanding the many facets of the new life in Christ. Each author approaches the same truth in a slightly different light which enables the reader to find someone who communicates in a manner that appeals to him. While I do not agree with everything in the recommended books (In fact, I don't agree with every thing I have written in the past!), each has something to offer which can be edifying to the discerning and Spirit-led reader.

Of course, no book or books can take the place of *The* Book, the Word of God, in the believer's life. I routinely recommend that a believer immerse himself in the truth of union with Christ by reading on successive days, Romans 6,7,8, Galatians, Ephesians, Philippians, and Colossians. In these passages, the instruction is to search out and underline all mentions of anything which speaks of our oneness or union with Christ–such phrases as: "in Him", "in whom", "in the beloved", "crucified with him", etc. It is well to rotate through these passages daily in your devotions, one passage per day, for several 5-day periods and meditate upon them.

As you abide in Him and His Word abides in you, you can expect that you will bring forth much fruit (John 15:5). And, you can expect to be resisted by the enemy of souls as you become effective in walking in the Spirit and leading others into freedom through the Cross. But, even in this, we have His unfailing promise, "For whatsoever is born of God overcometh the world: and this is the victory that overcometh the world, even our faith. Who is he that overcometh the world, but he that believeth that Jesus is the Son of God?" (1 John 5:4,5) And in 1 John 4:4: "Ye are of God, little children, and have overcome them: because greater is he that is in you than he that is in the world."

"And now, brethren, I commend you to God, and to the word of his grace, which is able to build you up, and to give you an inheritance among all them which are sanctified." (Acts 20:31)

PART II
A Spiritual Clinic For Your Church

INTRODUCTION

At the end of the 20th century, the church may be facing its greatest challenge since the Dark Ages. With humanism and secularism rampant on every hand, only a revived church will be able to withstand the onslaught and mount an offensive to recapture lost ground.

Many books are published which take into consideration methods, strategies, innovations and church growth; but few make the message of the Cross and revival central to the methods and goals. Great churches are not necessarily those with the largest numbers and mammoth facilities; relatively small churches have been known to have a significant impact on large numbers of people, many of whom may never enter the building or even be in the same vicinity. *True success on the part of the church will be measured in lives of believers transformed by the Spirit of God—not in reformation or conformation to a particular style of ministry or set of dogma, however evangelical.*

The purpose of PART II is to take a close look at the heart of the church and to help the reader assess what is of the flesh and what is of the Spirit in his own life and fellowship. It is intended that it be evaluative—not critical—and that each believer, especially those in leadership, may be spurred to prayer and action that the Holy Spirit may move in revival power.

RIVERSIDE
BAPTIST

N. Balkonski

CHAPTER I
THE CHURCH AND I–
A Sentimental Journey

Recently, the Lord has led my wife, Sue, and I to unite with Riverside Baptist Church in Denver where Dr. Rick Ferguson became pastor in January of 1991. Since I began ministry in 1970 I have wanted to be part of a fellowship which was committed to minister to believers that they might know the Lord Jesus Christ not only as Savior and Lord but, also, as Life. Under the leadership of Dr. Ferguson, this is now a reality. How I praise the Lord for my pastor's commitment to the Lord Jesus Christ and to winning the lost and edifying believers that they might mature in their walk in Christ! The initial steps have been taken, and it is anticipated that training at Riverside will continue that there may be those who will be able to help believers in various stages of growth from new birth, to the walk in the Spirit, and to being vitally involved in the ministry of the body.

First Baptist of Atlanta, under the ministry of Dr. Charles Stanley, inaugurated such a program in 1982; and it is being mightily used of God in the preparation of lay counselors and the development of believers. The materials contained in the PERSONAL SPIRITUAL CLINIC along with other materials developed by GFI are the core of the lay counseling training. As the ministry is developed at Riverside it will probably be along very similar lines with discipleship being given equal billing with evangelism. While I am satisfied with my church life presently, this has not always been the case. This is not to say that Riverside Baptist is the perfect church or that this teaching is fully in place, but it is taking a new direction that should result in God's working deeply in many lives.

Every believer has a story to tell regarding his introduction to the church in its local expression—usually a building with a name to distinguish it from many others very similar to it and a group of people who may take the name of the particular denomination. (I had one lady in counseling who told me that she was Second Baptist!) Though we call a group of believers a local church, there may be many ways in which it falls short of being a true New Testament church.

The true Church is triumphant, and the gates of Hell shall not prevail against it (Matt. 16:18); nothing that I write regarding the shortcomings of the local church should be construed as being said of the true church or Body of Christ for which He died. All Bible-believing churches will have some of the attributes of the Body of Christ, but all fall short in some particulars. We will be looking at the church in the early part of the book as an *organization* and in the latter part as an *organism*. It is the church as an *organism* that is the Body of Christ.

Even though the basic doctrines may be taught, the lost won to Christ, and some degree of discipleship carried out, there are many today inside the church who are floundering in their Christian walk who lament with the Psalmist, "I looked on my right hand, and beheld, but there was no man that would know me: refuge failed me; *no man cared for my soul*". (Ps. 142:4)

I will not repeat my personal testimony since I have detailed it elsewhere (*The Ins and Out of Rejection*, pp. 87-107). However, I think it may be instructive to some who have had mostly wholesome and edifying experiences with the church and an encouragement to others who have been disappointed, to walk through my life as I related to several churches. I do not hold these experiences to be normative, but many will agree that there have been such experiences in their backgrounds that have shaped their lives–either positively or negatively.

I have counseled with believers who are not in the church today because of some hurt inflicted upon them by other believers, many of whom did not even know they had been responsible for destruction in the life of another. Some have been severely wounded through church splits where they saw the family of God torn asunder with brother pitted against brother–sometimes brothers in the same earthly family.

As I detail some of the shortcomings in the church as I experienced it, you will realize that, as an adult in the church, I was equally to blame because there were those who looked to me as part of the church that let *them* down. In fact, during some of my worst suffering with emotional problems, I was chairman of the deacons in my church! Can you see that my own pain would have made me insensitive to the pain in others? But I am getting ahead of the story; let's go back to some beginnings in the early 30's in East Tennessee.

Since we lived on my grandmother's farm which was remote from any church and we had no automobile, we were obliged to walk a good distance to church most of the time. It was a rural church, obviously; and the pastors who were assigned to it were probably not the most experienced or educated that the denomination had to offer. It was evangelical and fundamental; I just couldn't comprehend the fundamentals!

Of course, all denominations have changed in the more than 50 years that I am recounting with many taking a turn for the worse; and I do not know to what extent this particular church was faithful to the doctrines extant at that time. My main recollection of the times in the church was the attendance of meetings which were typically called 'revivals'. These were typically held in the summer and were typified by 'Hell-fire and brimstone' preaching; at least, this is what stands out in bold relief in my mind. Don't misunderstand me; I thoroughly believe that Hell is as truly a place to be shunned as Heaven is a place to be gained. However, when you are regularly dangled over the pits of Hell and do not find the answer to avoid it, that is the *pits*! Amidst all of this, there were usually those who 'testified' of their new birth to spur on others to faith; would to God that we saw this more regularly in our churches today.

You see; I had heard the basics of the gospel, but I could not put it together in my young mind. I think you can see the effect that such a presentation would have had on an impressionable child and the fear and trauma which could ensue. I would see others 'go forward' to kneel at the mourner's bench and pray until they 'got it'. I distinctly remember my great aunt going to the bench and praying with many others kneeling around her, and she prayed until she shouted. To the great joy of those around her, she had 'got it'. I do not have any reason to doubt that she was truly born again, but the lesson I learned was that one had to tarry and pray until he shouted; otherwise, they were not born again (or *'borned again'* as so many said at that time).

While all of this was going on inside the 'church

house', there was usually a group of teenagers outside during the meetin' who were demonstrating their independence and/or rebellion by refusing to come inside. I was too young at the time to join them, but one can imagine some of the activities (dirty jokes, etc.) that claimed their attention. But the windows were open, and they assimilated some of the 'goings on' by osmosis. At least, they all knew that one of these days they must be 'borned again'; that is more than we can say for the average teenager today! They were going to put it off as long as possible, but all knew that one day they must 'get right' with the Lord.

I endured a number of those meetin's and several very similar in other settings, all of which were called 'revivals'. I have no recollection of a true revival ever having taken place, but they faithfully scheduled at least one a year and are still doing so to this day in many places in the South. Frequently, there were a number of souls saved; and the story went around that we really had revival! How can you have revival when you have not yet had 'vival (life)? True revival is for believers–not for the lost. Evangelistic meetings can be scheduled by men, but revival is sent by the Holy Spirit in answer to believing prayer and repentance.

Another 'revival' I attended and where I went down the 'sawdust trail' was conducted in a tent by an evangelist who had a second grade education. Though he faithfully proclaimed the gospel, and I went down the 'sawdust trail' to the makeshift altar, I went away lost another time as had become my practice. You see; people got down on their knees and prayed or mourned or something; but no one explained the gospel to me personally that I might understand and be saved.

Another venue in which the gospel was clearly proclaimed and in which I should have been saved was a small fundamental church in the community in which I was reared. The Holy Spirit was clearly in evidence that night, and I was spellbound by the youth evangelist who held the meetings. As I see it in retrospect, I was clearly being drawn by the Holy Spirit to make a surrender to the Lord Jesus Christ. However, there was the usual hitch when it came to 'invitation' time. The young evangelist took a different tack in making the call for the young people to come to Christ. He asked all of the Christians to come up and stand on one side and all of the non-Christians to come and stand on the other. In other words, he was dividing the sheep and the goats; and I was not *about* to be a goat! I saw my best friend making his way to stand with the 'sheep', and I knew I was just as good a kid as he so I went up and took my place as a 'sheep'. I am convinced in my heart that this is when I should have been saved, and possibly I was by taking my stand for Jesus with the 'sheep'. God knew that in my heart I wanted to know Him, even though I found it difficult to learn the way from His people.

After a number of 'false starts' such as this, I gave up on finding God in church and began to seek him in the privacy of my home. In all of my seeking, I was not exposed to anyone who could be termed a 'soul winner'; in that time and milieu, one was supposed to find Christ in 'revival meetin's' so far as I could figure out–*first you pray and then you shout!* Well, I determined one night at about the age of 17 that I was going to pray in my bed until the Lord showed me I was saved. I do not know how long I prayed, but after a while I had a peace given by the Spirit that I was His child. Now, I can shout, "Hallelujah!"; but I did not shout at the time, contrary to the scene to which I had been exposed. You can see that the stage was set for me to doubt my salvation due to lack of solid scriptural foundation and proper discipleship; in my case this was augmented by deep-seated emotional problems which caused me to feel unsaved, as well.

Some form of discipleship would have been in order at this time, but that was not to be. Since everyone thought I was a Christian anyway, I saw no reason to make it public. By this time, we had been in a small church for about 10 years. I can remember joining the church at the age of 6 with my parents answering some questions for me and some water being sprinkled on my head. As I understand it now, there should have been a time around age 12 when I answered the questions for myself, but that sort of got lost in the shuffle. You see, our pastor had 4 or 5 other churches (a circuit); and he had little time for adults, much less for children. We had 'preaching' on the first Sunday morning and third Sunday night of the month. Of course, 'revivals' which never materialized were regularly scheduled there, too. I recall, though, one of the godly pastors, Rev. Willis Johnson, placing his hand on my head on the front porch of the church once and telling my parents that I was going to be used of the Lord. It may have been a passing statement for him, or he may have had the witness of the Spirit that this was to be the case; in either event, it has remained in my memory for more than 55 years.

I attended church regularly and started to college shortly after I was saved. This was in 1947 immediately following World War II, and I had two veterans for roommates with a number of other veterans for friends. Needless to say, I grew up very rapidly in the ensuing months; I was 17, and they had been through a war–early 20's going on 35! Though I attended church some during college, there is nothing in the four years that stands out in my memory where I was challenged to grow in Him. I do not blame this on anyone; I should have been searching for a church which would minister to my needs in some way.

After my wife, Sue, and I were married at age 20 and relocated to Baltimore at age 21, we joined a church where we were fairly active. The pastor was a godly man who preached the Word; but there was little, if any, spiritual growth at that time. I did go on a retreat with the men of the church where there was a solid challenge to commitment by a Bishop Raines. Even though this was a very turbulent time in my life, emotionally and spiritually, I was not able to put it all together in a manner which would have any great effect on my life.

At the age of 27 and 3 children later, still not having found how to do business with God in church and being at the point of desperation, I went to my bedroom again (this time in Baltimore) and totally sold out to the Lord Jesus Christ; but, as before, I didn't tell anyone about it. You would think I would have learned to let someone in on the secret that they might be of help; I guess I expected them to read my mind and take the initiative. We transferred to another church of the same stripe about this time, and I became very active. I realize now that it was much ado about nothing, but it was all I knew to do at the time. There was one brother with whom I shared at some depth, but he did not know how to point me to the fulfillment I was needing and seeking (in all of the wrong places).

At the age of 29 (1959) I accepted a transfer to Denver with Martin Marietta Corporation; and we asked God to show us where we should worship. A friend had left the name of a church on my desk at work, and we decided to try it. After a couple of months we joined and were baptized in a fundamental church. The teaching was sound, and the people were friendly. Having great needs within which were never expressed to those in leadership (or anyone else for that matter), I plunged in headlong and became hyperactive. Of course, new blood is always welcome; and I was promptly given work to do. Even though I had a severe inferiority complex as described in my complete testimony in *Ins and Out of Rejection*, I forced myself to do some teaching and, eventually, some 'deking'; and, after a period of time, I learned to do some soul winning. I had come to believe that soul winning was more or less the pinnacle of Christian service (and growth!). However, there was still something missing in my spiritual life that I could not define and didn't know where to look for an answer.

The "Unknown Christian" in *How to Live the Victorious Life* gives this personal testimony, "As the writer looks back on his past life nothing so surprises him as the fact that he failed to see, or grasp, or apprehend this Victorious Life teaching, although it is not new, although it is so plainly taught in Scripture". I'm glad I am not the only one to have had that experience!

There was a brother in the church whom I greatly admired and with whom I shared to some extent; he was walking with the Lord and even had joy! There was, however, a major problem; he had what I needed, but he didn't know what he had! You see; he had a major life transformation at salvation but didn't understand the extent of what God had done. He, too, was like the "Unknown Christian". His name is John Stevens, and you will have to know a little more about John to appreciate what I am recounting. You can get to know him much better through his fine book, *Suicide, An Illicit Lover*, available from GFI.

During the period from 1959 to 1965, I am sure that John (and, perhaps, others) prayed for me in *self-defense*; but neither he, the pastor, others, nor myself, recognized the depth of my problems. You see, I had the ability to put on a front or mask and become deeply involved in the Lord's (?) work and make the effort to work out my problem on someone else by staying busy in various kinds of service. Sound familiar? It is not that I did not love the Lord and or that His work was not going on in that church; *the problem was that I was* doing *in order to* be *because I didn't know how to* be *in order to* do! In other words, I didn't know who I was in Christ and was trying to build an identity in the church based on service or doing–performance based acceptance.

Though I was not consciously being hypocritical and God was honoring all of the effort that was of Him, I was running out of steam; and I knew it. However, I did not know what to do about it. I couldn't take on more work in the church because all of my time was taken now, and my energy level would not permit it if I could have. By this time I had been elected chairman of the deacons (which I needed like another hole in my head!) Shortly after my election, my anxiety level began to increase until I was back on medication as I had been in my 20's. This time, the medication was for pain in my head instead of my stomach; however, the source of both was the flesh or self-centered life which was yet to be diagnosed and treated by the Holy Spirit.

By October 1965, I was at the end of my rope (anxiety neurosis according to the world system) as is explained in my more complete testimony; and God did a deeper work in my life, using the truth contained in the following verse:

"I am crucified with Christ: nevertheless I live; yet not I, but Christ liveth in me: and the life which I now live in the flesh I live by the faith of the Son of God, who loved me, and gave himself for me." (Galatians 2:20)

The following Sunday, I 'went forward' to give public testimony that God had met me in a new way. I was finally taking the step of letting other believers know that there was a new beginning. As I recall, I was not permitted to speak at any length to explain as best I could what God had shown me. This being the case, there was no one who offered counsel on how to walk in the new life and to show me the pitfalls of the victorious life. (See *Victory in Christ*, last chapter, by Charles Trumbull). Though I studied extensively in Paul's letters and read many biographies (including *Hudson Taylor's Spiritual Secret*) and autobiographies in the ensuing year, I was down more than I was up for the next two years as I learned how to walk in the Spirit as much by trial and error as from the Word of God. The reading of these different authors showed me some patterns that were common to all; most had experienced a period of deep anxiety prior to coming to know Christ as their very Life (See *Crowded to Christ* by L. E. Maxwell). Despite my spiritual hardheadedness I didn't lack tenacity, and I began to level out in a more consistent walk; about two years later, God called me to the ministry of counseling using the verses, Isaiah 58:10,11:

"And if thou draw out thy soul to the hungry, and satisfy the afflicted soul; then shall thy light rise in obscurity, and thy darkness be as the noon day: And the Lord shall guide thee continually, and satisfy thy soul drought, and make fat thy bones: and thou shalt be like a watered garden, and like a spring of water whose waters fail not." (Isa. 58:10,11)

In addition to my study in the Word, I began to pursue a Master's degree at the University of Colorado which was awarded in December 1969. During the early months of 1969, John Stevens asked me to teach his Sunday School class. I thought it was only right that I should share with him that which I intended to teach, so we went to a restaurant where I drew some crude diagrams on a napkin. As I sketched it out John exclaimed, "That's what happened to me!" To which I replied, "Thanks a *lot*, buddy!" When I met John 10 years earlier, all of this had been true in his life, but he didn't know what he had and was unable to share it with me. Therefore, I went through the 'tortures of the damned' for another 6 years after I met John even though he was living the life that God was bringing to pass in my experience. He was a more mature believer at the time and still is, but he could not articulate the way to victory to another as he does so effectively now. Shortly after that time, John agreed to be on the founding board of directors of Grace Fellowship International (GFI) to help in disseminating the message of the Cross worldwide.

As Chairman of the Deacons, John was instrumental in leading the church to license me to the Gospel Ministry of Counseling. However, the leadership of the church as a whole did not recognize the extent of the ministry to which God was calling me. I am certain that I didn't live the life as consistently as I desired, but I believe the scripture still holds true that a 'prophet' is not usually accepted in his own home town (or home church). Though the pastors were supportive to some degree, I was never allowed to give a systematic presentation to the church of that which God had taught me in order that some of the brothers and sisters might have been spared some of the years of agony through which I had gone–alone. Too, they were not able to understand my need for prayer personally and in the developing ministry.

We were members of this local church for almost 32 years, but I had very little visibility even though I ministered internationally beginning in 1978. Partially because of this, the local Christian educational institutions tended not to take the counseling approach too seriously. What a different story it could have been had my pastors been led of the Lord to run some interference for me with the Christian establishment and to help me from the beginning with my faults (which were legion) and with my walk and work. That local church could have been used of God in training pastors from around the country and from other countries to help believers with just such internal problems as I had to battle through, between me and the Lord, in silence and tears.

I am not faulting the people of that church; after all, they had to put up with me! While I was going through all of the learning process, I was undoubtedly oblivious to the internal struggles of others who were going through similar or worse difficulties than I. In fact, my responsibility was greater because I was one of the leaders to whom they should have been able to turn.

In all of this, my Lord has been more than sufficient; may His name be praised! My purpose in sharing this is to act as an advocate for the millions of believers who are in local fellowships of believers, Sunday after Sunday, sitting there in silent desperation, not knowing where to turn. *Brethren, this ought not so to be*! The Word says we are to love the Lord with all our heart, mind, soul, and strength and our neighbor as ourselves. How can we love the Lord in this way without being committed to each other and knowing who we are in Christ?

Many of the believers who are having the greatest struggles have the greatest potential in God's Kingdom, but who is going to stand in the gap for them and lead them out of the Wilderness into Canaan (from defeat into victory)? How many times do we hear those, both in the pulpit and the pew, speak of 'back door revivals' where the troublemakers are ushered from the nurture of the Body of Christ to find their own way in the cold, cruel world? Surely, such believers are a pain in the body (in more ways than one!); but many are so desperate they are just on the brink of finding a deepened relationship with the Lord if someone would only believe *in* them and *for* them while they flounder in the Wilderness approaching Jordan. The problem is that, all too frequently, both the *helper* and the *helpee* may be floundering on the same side of Jordan–the side of the Wilderness and defeat! And, those who are not may be like my good friend, John Stevens was for a period of time; they may have the victory that a desperate person needs but be unable to lead him across the Jordan to the promised rest. (Heb. 4:9,10)

All of these experiences, the bad and the good, are used of God to draw us to Himself and to conform us to His image (Rom. 8:28,29). *Failure, Back Door to Success*, by Dr. Erwin Lutzer shows how some of the negative experiences of life may be used by God to great advantage in our lives.

After God's calling me to the ministry in 1967, it was necessary to obtain the credentials which would convince others (at least a few) that I was equipped to begin a ministry of counseling. Though the master's degree was insufficient, it was awarded in December 1969; and the Lord provided me with a layoff from industry which permitted me to begin counseling in my basement at home February 1, 1970. There was no promise of financial support from any individual or church; it was both a faith venture and a world vision from the inception. Faithful to His calling and honoring His infallible Word, the Holy Spirit began to transform lives; and, beginning in August of 1972, other staff members were added. The first major book, *Handbook to Happiness* (Tyndale House) was published in early 1972 with the next, *The Ins and Out of Rejection*, following in 1975; *Counseling with the Mind of Christ* (Revell) was published in 1978 and *The Rejection Syndrome* (Tyndale) in 1982.

It was necessary first to prove that this method of communicating revival to the hearts and lives of believers was not unique to myself. This had been established with the early staff members, but the remote training had to be developed which would permit outlying offices to be opened. The first was in 1975, and others were added in the early 80's. The first international office was established in 1981 with God's calling Guillermo Donamaria, M.D., to be our Latin American director, with headquarters in Rosario, Argentina. In 1982, the work was launched in India under the direction of Professor P. P. Thomas who, along with his staff, has done extensive training in various parts of his country.

A great number of spin-off ministries have been spawned over the years, some of which have a particular emphasis, but the central focus on the teaching of the Cross or the exchanged life is common to all. In 1986, Grace Fellowship International was decentralized, making the former branch offices into independent entities which were authorized to use GFI materials within their own ministries. This has resulted in multiplication of the message and the freedom to develop along lines which make maximum utilization of the spiritual gifts and abilities of the personnel in the particular office.

In God's sovereignty, He called GFI into being for a particular purpose–to demonstrate the practicality of communicating revival to defeated and hurting believers on a one-on-one basis. That has been proven over and over again in this and other countries and languages by lay believers with little or no education in counseling, as well as with professionals who have been willing to submit to the Holy Spirit's transforming work in their own lives. Recently, a 56 year old farmer from Australia came to Colorado for a short period of training–about two weeks. He did not have a high school education but had been discipled for a period of time by a representative of the Navigators. He lost his wife after 6 years with cancer; and, upon his return from the States, a lady came to him for counseling who had recently lost her mother to cancer. The loss of his wife and the recent training allowed him to share with her in such a way that resulted in her finding radical victory after having angrily forsaken her walk with God for a period of time.

Innumerable believers who had been treated unsuccessfully by psychologists and psychiatrists have found healing and wholeness as the Holy Spirit renewed their minds and transformed their lives–a vivid description of revival. The Holy Spirit performs miracles–psychiatrists, psychologists, and counselors, even though Christian, do not. Others were believers who were defeated in life and ministry because of attempting to live and minister in the pulpit, pew, or on the mission field in the strength of the flesh. This was due to their not having been taught, or they had not caught, the way to appropriate their new life in Christ.

Had the church been carrying out its God-given

mandate, GFI would never have been called into being. I am praying that enough churches will respond to the challenge to minister the message of the Cross that the specialized ministry of GFI would no longer be needed. When that takes place the mission of GFI will have been accomplished.

I am fully convinced that the church has never ceased to be God's priority and that its being anemic and all but impotent in many of its manifestations or its local expressions has not deterred God from His original plan: ". . . Christ also loved the church, and gave himself for it; That he might sanctify and cleanse it with the washing of water by the word, that he might present it to himself a glorious church, not having spot, or wrinkle, or any such thing; that it should be holy and without blemish" (Eph. 5:25b-27).

As I approach Chapter 3 and do a sort of *post-mortem*, it is the earthly organization to which I am referring–not the heavenly organism described by the Word of God as the church triumphant. With this crucial distinction in mind, let us investigate the *status quo* which someone has aptly defined as Latin for 'the mess we are in'! But, prior to looking at the church, let's look at the society to which it is called upon to minister–a society characterized by consummate selfishness. Many churches are continuing to minister with a mentality and methods appropriate to the 50's which are all but irrelevant to where people are today. As a result, they frequently find themselves answering questions that people are not asking! The message, the centrality of the Cross of Christ, must never change; however, we must communicate it in such a way as to be understood by those whom we would reach. It is my prayer that the suggestions offered in the latter part of this book will be used of God in helping to rectify this situation.

CHAPTER II
THE WORK OF THE CHURCH:
Ministering to a Selfish and Sin-sick Society

It should be patently obvious that taking a self-sacrificing gospel to a self-indulgent population is going to be met with stiff resistance. Selfism is firmly entrenched in the very existence of individuals and institutions in this country and has invaded the church in insidious ways. What's in it for me? and instant gratification are keystones to understanding that which is appealing to the rank and file sinner and all too many blood-bought believers who have been reared in a permissive and indulgent society. Believers who have not been divested of the ways of the self-life (flesh) will necessarily take these with them into the sanctuary and into the various activities of the church. For example, good business practices will help the church to do things decently and in order which is scriptural. However, it would be possible to employ such business practices in the decision-making process of the church to the exclusion of seeking God's directive will in all decisions. Many other such examples could be cited where the church may tend to lean on the arm of the flesh rather than employing the spiritual gifts of believers in carrying out the work of the Spirit.

It is necessary to take a look at what selfism has done to society as a whole before we can appreciate its encroachments into the life and ministry of the church in all too many areas. Of course, the American ideal of individualism has its part to play in the development of a society that refuses to sacrifice individual comfort in the interest of the common good. And the work ethic which has been bedrock in the building of our nation has been carried over into the church in some unhealthy ways. Yes, we are ". . . created *in Christ Jesus* unto good works, which God hath before ordained that we should walk in them". (Eph. 2:10) The key to this passage is that the good works are to be done *in Christ* not in the strength of the flesh, or in the resources of the self-centered life, which is so frequently overlooked or misunderstood.

We have a generation which has not known hardship and which has come to expect a continuously expanding economy. That expectation has been fueled since World War II to the point that Baby Boomers or those who can not recall the deprivation of the Great Depression are inclined to believe that prosperity is their due. Some groups have even made this integral to the preaching of their 'gospel'. Can you imagine preaching to impoverished believers in Ethiopia that they can claim as their spiritual birthright a new Cadillac? (Of course, they might pray for a dune buggy!) Or to believers in Eastern Europe that the affluence of their brethren in America can be theirs from God merely by claiming it? Does God love us more than He does believers in countries where they are literally trusting God for their daily bread? Or, is it likely that we may yet go through some of the privation that they are presently experiencing?

It is not too difficult to adjust to an expanding economy where things are getting better and better; it can be extremely cramping to one's style to adjust to one where things are getting worse and worse! One has only to observe the effects of the shrinking economy that are nipping at the heels of many to extrapolate to that which will be the case, if and when further erosions of the economy are suffered.

Some middle-aged corporate executives who have been accustomed to generous salaries and have built a life style accordingly, have found themselves unemployed due to a corporate merger which deleted their position. Some have found themselves in the unenviable position of driving to a church in a Mercedes to obtain groceries from the food basket! It has become the rule rather than the exception to leverage one's income and buy housing and other things thought to be necessities by incurring inordinate installment debt. Losing the income totally or having an extended period of unemployment followed by accepting a lesser salary can mean the loss of assets, identity, bankruptcy, or even suicide. Some have even joined the ranks of the homeless after having enjoyed a considerable degree of comfort.

During the term of economic expansion, workers began to demand more and more in salary and benefits through coercion by strikes which caused an upward spiral in prices and an unfavorable comparison with goods from other countries where selfishness had not reached the same proportions or was manifested in different ways.

One has only to look at the steel industry to see how we have shot ourselves in the foot. We priced ourselves out of the market and put an inordinate portion of the revenue into wages and 13 week vacations without plowing back a sufficient amount into upgrading the facilities and equipment. Now, other countries have outstripped us in production using state of the art equipment and processes which makes us dependent upon foreign steel with the concomitant loss of jobs and ripple effect into other industries–particularly the automotive industry.

We can see the same situation with the garment industry where thousands of jobs have been lost in this country because of lower wages in Third World countries. Impacted in another way is agribusiness where the cost for durable goods and wages have all but made the family farm an impossibility. Though his costs have multiplied, the income per bushel for wheat or corn has not risen accordingly. This squeeze can not continue indefinitely if the populace is to eat; *if the farmer gets too hungry, you can bet that he will not be by himself!*

The rising costs have made it all but impossible for a family to live on one income if they are to avail themselves of all of the things and commodious housing to which they have been accustomed or to which they believe they are entitled. Most young people want to begin their married lives having the same housing, furnishings and automobiles which their parents have spent most of a lifetime in amassing. Installment debt makes this possible, but the down side is that servicing debt prevents preparation for the children's education and other activities that would enhance family togetherness. Also, continuous financial pressure takes its toll on the marital relationship. Many families are on the brink of bankruptcy which a short interruption in income can easily precipitate. This has been demonstrated in thousands of homes in recent years.

Some who have known the security that finances can bring have been thrown into pandemonium by the failure of banks and insurance companies which have traditionally been trusted servants. Dishonesty in handling pension funds or the bankruptcy of a company where a person may have worked for most of a lifetime can destroy the hope of a secure retirement literally overnight.

Rampant dishonesty in the handling of funds in banking, insurance companies or corporate financing have made 'doing business as usual' an unusual occurrence. The moral fabric of the country has all but come unravelled and is heading downhill at a breakneck pace! In years gone by, a person's word was his bond; and transactions were based on honesty and integrity as compared with today's sham and deceit. Many start businesses on borrowed money and take funds for personal use, knowing that, if they can't make a go of it, they can always take bankruptcy. Individuals run up staggering amounts on credit cards and take bankruptcy, leaving institutions and individuals holding the bag with little or no remorse.

In a society which is no longer built on absolutes, there is no firm foundation on which a person may build a life, vocation or family because everything is subject to change without notice. In a recent issue of *Moody Monthly*, it was stated that 6 out of 10 children born since 1980 will spend part of their developmental years in a single parent home. Children who yet have both parents may derive more of their values from the world system through television than from that which was the upbringing of their parents. Between television and peer pressure, our young people do not have a fighting chance without the direct intervention of the Spirit of God.

As societal values continue to erode and the family structure disintegrates, a severely shrinking economy (which is projected by many economists) could have a catastrophic effect. In the Depression of the '30s, those who were fortunate enough to have something extra shared with those who didn't. They pulled together so that, in many instances, families and farms were kept from going under. The selfism of the present age would militate against such a scenario except in isolated situations. Given a similar set of circumstances, it is much more likely that rioting and looting would occur as the 'have-nots' rob and plunder those who yet have possessions. Were that to happen today, no residence would be safe unless guarded continuously. As you may remember, a few years ago there was rioting in the streets of London and wanton burning of vehicles because of unemployment. There was not even the thought of working together to resolve the situation as the unemployed were demanding immediate gratification of their desires and resorting to violence when that was not forthcoming.

Privation is not easy for anyone, especially for those who have never been called upon to endure it. However, it is becoming more commonplace among groups and countries which have traditionally been stable. Recent events in Europe and Russia have changed the face of that part of the world, and the political and economic systems which have been disrupted will continue to cause major repercussions for years to come.

Liberation Theology is being espoused in a number of Third World countries, beginning in Latin America and spreading to India and Africa to take advantage of the disadvantaged; using a 'humanistic gospel' with Marxist overtones as a rallying cry, cooperating churches are being used as outposts in most Latin American countries. With clerics writing the books on the subject, there are those who are duped into thinking there is something Christian about it. Such 'theology' further dilutes that which has historically been taught in those countries. Some of the funding of this movement has come from Marxist countries; with the fall of Communism and the reshaping of the Soviet Union, the 'offerings' may fall off considerably! For years the oppressed and/or minorities have been organized in various ways to throw off regimes which have ruled unfairly, or were so perceived, with other totalitarian governments put in their places; Liberation Theology is merely another ploy to accomplish the same thing by deception through the churches.

There is a generation in this country which has come to believe that the 'good life' is their birthright, and no one has the right to take it from them or to frustrate their plans that things should get better and better. As part of this package in the last 3 decades, free sex of any kind for anyone at any time and almost any place has been promoted as the *recreation* of choice without the responsibilities of *procreation*. Until 1973, homosexuality was officially a mental illness and abortion was murder; in that watershed year, both were legitimized without reference to the absolutes of God's Word. Homosexuals brought pressure to bear on the behavioral sciences to delete this perversion from their taxonomy of mental illness and went on to secure civil rights for their sin. Women were led to believe that the right of choice about the extinguishing of a life was theirs–not God's. Untold millions (almost twice the population of Australia) of babies have been killed in America, the land of the free and the home of protected murder, and the mothers suffer the consequences of their sin in guilt and psychological pathology.

Add to all of this the destruction in lives and families caused by alcohol, drugs and the AIDS plague, and it becomes obvious that we have human need of mammoth proportions. The mental health system has all but broken down under its own weight, and the government and insurance financing to treat the symptoms of the rampant human misery is rapidly drying up. Those who have depended upon the devices invented by man (therapies) to assuage the symptomatology created by violating God's absolutes will now have nowhere to turn except *inward* or *upward*. However, the upward look must be facilitated by God's people in the church; and the church is not exactly coping well with its own shortcomings! The added burden of the onslaught of those suffering from mental, emotional and behavioral problems, which is certain to come, will serve to reveal the incompetency of the average church to minister in the Spirit to problems for which the flesh has no answers. In other words, the cover is about to be blown revealing to the world what it had long suspected; in the face of overwhelming need, the resources of the average church will be taxed beyond their limits.

Meanwhile, the average church on the corner is going about its concerns (or unconcerns) conducting business as usual, causing the world to question its relevancy when the chips are down! The fleshly ministry of the average church is about as effective as charging Hell with a water pistol! If this were not the case, the number of churches in this country could have a revolutionary effect on the immoral tide that is sweeping this country into the garners of the cults, the occult, Islam, New Age and any other thing that is contrary to sound doctrine. Because many believers are not discipled and grounded in their faith, some are deceived by false doctrine and are led into heresy; and others fall by the wayside and make shipwreck of their faith.

Turning the tide in this country will require that believers quit 'playing church' and get serious about the Lordship of Jesus Christ. This means that we must take a serious view of sin and its consequences, both here and hereafter. True believers know that Holy Spirit revival is the only answer, and God will send it if we meet His requirements:

CHAPTER II

"If my people, which are called by my name, shall humble themselves, and pray, and seek my face, and turn from their wicked ways; then will I hear from heaven, and will forgive their sin, and will heal their land." (2 Chronicles 7:14)

CHAPTER III
THE STATE
OF THE CHURCH–
A Post Mortem

I realize that the church is not *totally* without life, but there are many signs of death–at least in its incipient stages. Usually, a person who is dying is in pain and is not extremely aware of, or concerned about, the difficulty and conflict being experienced by those around him. Too, he is typically not reproducing himself and being a major force in edifying those who have been dependent upon him. Any thinking person will agree that the church is no longer a force with which to be reckoned as it was in the early days of our country. Though it has not ceased to function, much of the *activity* is without *productivity*; and many of the same programs would continue, with about the same results, if the Holy Spirit departed. Our churches must be transfused with new life if we are to see the teeming millions come to Christ and if Christians are to have a testimony that will attract the lost to Christ and His Church.

In many churches today, the results of evangelism may be minimal with only a few being saved, and these are frequently children; some evangelical churches do not see one person saved in an entire year. This is not to disparage the winning of children to the Lord since a small percentage are saved after they are adults. However, there are churches that are doing a

105

good job of evangelism who are doing little, if anything, in discipleship or edification of those who are won to the Lord. Extremely rare in this country is the church where all new believers are offered the option of one-on-one and group discipleship that they might be thoroughly grounded in the faith.

The churches which are experiencing the most growth are not necessarily reaching the greatest numbers for Christ; many are merely shuffling God's people from one building to another. In fact, some of those with stupendous growth from a numerical standpoint are flooded with members from other churches who are desirous of being lost in the crowd, and the bigger the better, since that makes it all the easier to hide! I have had a number of people in counseling admit they went to a larger church because they did not want to get 'involved'. Hiding from God in the church makes a person much harder to find since he looks much like all of the others, many of whom are playing the same game! The camouflage of being a church member and attending at least one service each week tends to fend off the faithful and assuage his conscience by maintaining the facade of spirituality. The new phenomenon, the Mega church, is tailor made for just such a person; he can fill the pew without being close to being filled with the Spirit or, sometimes, even coming to grips with his emptiness! Entertainment is high on the agenda in many such churches, and personal growth and edification often take a back seat to the 'success' criteria.

In more than two decades of counseling with people inside and outside the church, it is very common to hear them say, "I just don't know where to turn!". Frequently, these words are uttered by those who are active, or even leading, in a Bible-believing church.

Many have sought answers to their problems by burying themselves in the work of the church which seems to suffice for a while. Others have assiduously followed the advice of trusted leaders and have kept the standards required to be a 'good Christian'. Some have become involved in open sin and have made shipwreck of their lives, while a host of others settle for a mediocrity of Christian experience which does not have the stamp of God upon it. While not all would have responded to godly counsel or discipleship in the early years of their Christian experience, a significant percentage would have, had such edification been readily available.

Pastors who have unresolved issues in their own lives are frequently trapped since an admission of need is tantamount to an admission of failure. Some suffer in silence until they become disenchanted with the ministry and just go through the motions or burn out; or, in some cases, they become involved in wanton sin and lose their ministries and, sometimes, their families. It is absolutely necessary that pastors have access to an accepting relationship where they can evaluate their own spiritual growth without the stigma of being thought 'mentally ill' or their fitness for ministry being brought into question unless, of course, there is a moral issue with which they must deal.

If a pastor begins to come to the end of himself as did Hudson Taylor on the mission field, he could be on the verge of becoming the greatest pastor the church has ever had. However, it is common that neither he nor the church leadership recognizes the opportunity of the situation to get a new pastor in the same physical body! That being the case, the pulpit committee gets very active and decides that the pastor can get help elsewhere while they search for another who is is a little higher on the backside of the crest of the wave but still on his way down! The pastor is only guilty of being a person with whom God must deal just as He does the rest of us! Many excellent candidates for the mission field are rejected because of personality disturbances which dealing with the self-life (flesh) would resolve. All too frequently, those sent out are psychologically well adjusted but may be no more spiritually mature than their less well adjusted brother or sister who was forced to stay home. In fact, the one with the greater problem has more motivation to find answers and could make the better missionary, were he given the opportunity.

Whether pastor or layman, the overwhelming tendency is to send them outside the church for help by individuals or organizations who hold themselves out to give 'Christian' answers. These may fall under the rubric of Christian psychology, Christian psychiatry, or a host of programs falling under the 12-step approach, adapted or adopted from Alcoholics Anonymous. Co-dependency, ACOA (Adult Child of Alcoholic) and other such terminology have proliferated and infiltrated the very ministry of the church.

Once the world system develops a new fad, it is not long until Christians pick it up and try to convert it for use in the church. Refusal to 'buy in' to the current counseling fad, slang or terminology tends to set one aside as being different or 'not really being with it'. However, I have found that fads come and go; but the Cross remains a constant!

Some believers do not stop and think that nineteen centuries of Christians were denied the genius of Freud and the dubious blessing of '12-step' programs; *the one step of coming to know the Lord Jesus Christ in His fullness seemed to be sufficient for first century Christians!* Though all of the approaches to helping people have some truth or they would not get off the ground at all, every thinking believer in assessing the doctrinal soundness of any form of teaching, especially the presuppositions of various forms of therapy, should ask the obvious question:

BUT WHERE IS THE CROSS?

There is a plethora of written material which is Christian, or which purports to be, that is woefully silent on the role of the Cross in the life of the believer. Some of this oversight may be by design, but much is due to the fact that the emphasis of the presentation is an aspect other than that where the Cross is traditionally brought into focus. In yesteryear when there was less liberalism, there was more material where the Cross stood out in bold relief; when it did not, it was assumed because a greater percentage of believers were able to 'read between the lines'.

Before I proceed further, I must stop and explain what I mean when I use the term, 'Cross'. I am not referring to the substitutionary work of the Lord Jesus Christ in the atonement for our sins. This is assumed as understood and appropriated by faith or else the person is not a believer and is yet "...dead in trespasses and sins...". (Eph. 2:1) One who is born of the Spirit has understood the truth of the Lord Jesus dying *for him* in the free pardon of sins–redemption or justification. And, positionally, he was united with the Lord Jesus in death and resurrection as is so clearly delineated in Romans 6. Though the work of the Cross *for* the believer has been accomplished for all eternity, the work of the Cross *in* the believer may not be understood nor appropriated in the life of the believer in all of his sojourn here on Earth. This faith appropriation in the believer's life may be termed sanctification or entering by faith into the reality of union with Christ in His death and resurrection, sometimes referred to as identification with Christ. Others might call it the filling of the Spirit, Lordship, the abiding life, the abundant life, the victorious life, the life of rest, the hidden life, the exchanged life or other terminology indicating that the Life of the Lord Jesus is lived out in the believer–not as a second work of grace but as a Spirit-given understanding of our inheritance in Christ.

I am fully aware of the theological bias that this view represents and that a great segment of Christianity, involving respected theologians of the past and present, would take issue–lovingly or otherwise. However, I do not hesitate to take my stand with such time-honored saints as J. Hudson Taylor, Andrew Murray, Madame Guyon, F.B. Meyer, Charles Trumbull, L.E. Maxwell, F.J. Huegel, Watchman Nee, A. T. Pierson, and a host of others. While some are adept at developing systems of theology which may or may not be blessed of the Lord, these were used of the Lord in bringing about the transformation of lives in the past; and their work goes on through their writings until the present time.

Though the believer has three enemies–the world, the flesh and the Devil, our prime focus here is the *flesh* and the deceptions which are perpetrated or accepted because of it. (The reader is directed to my booklet, *Gems and Jargon*, for an explanation of the difference between the flesh and the old man or sin nature). My thesis is that the flesh either has been (and is being) dealt with through the experienced Cross (Galatians 2:20), or it yet holds sway in the life of the believer. If the flesh holds sway, the believer may be a practicing theologian or a fervent lay person or a believer who has "...followed him afar off..."(Mark 14:54); in this sense, all may be deceived and may, unwittingly, practice deception. This is not to say that such believers are charlatans. J. Hudson Taylor was on the mission field for more than a decade before he experienced the work of the Cross in his own life–exchanging the self-life for the Christ-life. Indeed, most believers who are broken such that the Cross becomes an experiential reality in their lives have been believers several to many years.

But what is the point I am trying to make? Much of the prevalent teaching and writing falls short of making the experienced Cross explicit. Obviously, a theological system which denies the possibility of the Cross becoming an experiential reality would prevent its being understood in this sense. Then, those who do not hold alien theology but who, themselves, have not entered into the reality of it in experience can not teach it in a manner which leads to life. If death (the experiential understanding of the Cross) has not worked in them, then another kind of death (self-life or flesh, or being carnally minded) will work in others–the antithesis of: "So then death worketh in us, but life in you." (2 Cor. 4:12)

Not only will flesh be nurtured by the absence of the teaching of the Cross and prevent the believer from walking in victory; but, also, his ability to discern fleshly teaching and false doctrine is not developed. Or, this discernment is more of an intellectual and theological bent than it is spiritual. Lacking spiritual discernment, the theological positioning may be thoroughly orthodox while being spiritually lacking. Also, it is possible for the believer to be deceived by that which looks good but which has its basis in humanism, existentialism, New Age teaching or is the fleshly integration of secular facts with scriptural truth. Let's look at some of the contemporary, and biblical, teaching which falls short in some aspects. For example, there are many very good approaches to evangelism which are being honored by the Lord. Many are won to the Lord by understanding the death and resurrection of the Lord Jesus Christ for them but who are yet walking after the flesh or in their own strength. It is glorious that they may well be saved and going to Heaven but deplorable that so many will never know the victory that the scripture says is the birthright of every believer. Evangelism is scriptural, and the need for multiplying it is urgent and critical; BUT WHERE IS THE CROSS?

Again, there are many good approaches to discipleship which are instrumental in equipping believers in several particulars; BUT WHERE IS THE CROSS? The understanding of the experienced cross is conspicuously absent in most of the approaches to discipleship which are widely used by the church and para-church organizations today. This despite the truth of Luke 14:27: "And whosoever doth not bear his cross, and come after me, cannot be my disciple."

Believers with emotional conflict and problems with interpersonal problems are increasingly turning to Christian psychology and psychiatry for assistance. Many in those fields are extremely helpful in providing assistance to those who are hurting. Too, some of these attempt to make an assiduous application of scripture during the course of therapy to the situation, internal and external, with which the client is struggling. Application of scripture and of scriptural principles can be helpful, and God will honor it, BUT WHERE IS THE CROSS? Either the flesh is dealt with by the Cross or it is strengthened for its inevitable conflict with the Spirit (Gal. 5:17). It is not God's purpose that His Word should strengthen the flesh, but many are admonished diligently to keep the law and employ scriptural principles while not being taught to draw upon their resources in Christ to do so.

We are blessed with many good Christian educational institutions from kindergarten to graduate level instruction. Christian subjects are taught in Christian settings, BUT WHERE IS THE CROSS? Some would deny the efficacy of the Cross to deal with the flesh because of an incompatible theological system while others teach the truth in courses on sanctification but do not integrate it in other courses having to do with spiritual life. As a result, emotional and mental disturbances are often seen as being the domain of the behavioral scientist rather than being the opportunity for the application of the spiritual life to the spiritual need.

Due to the lack of emphasis on the teaching of the Cross, there is much false teaching that goes undetected; and believers are being deceived. A believer I met was in administration in a major Christian college for almost two decades when he was exposed to some teaching which had the appearance of truth. He was at the point of buying the tapes and becoming a distributor when he began to understand the truth of the Cross in his own life. Thus enlightened, he had the discernment given by the Spirit that the teaching which had sounded so good initially was, in reality, New Age heresy. The tenets of Hinduism can creep in obliquely and be appealing to the flesh and not be detected by the fleshly mind. Believers who have become accustomed to the absence of the Cross, as explicit teaching, do not have this as a yardstick by which to measure that with which they come into contact. The material may sound wonderful, BUT WHERE IS THE CROSS?

A believer may love the Lord and be engrossed in Christian service and have all the earmarks of a 'good

Christian'. He may have an identity shaped by the affluence of this country or by the suffering of the environment behind the Iron or Bamboo Curtain and yet be subtly dominated by the reign of the flesh. On the one hand, the flesh can be proud of its prosperity; or, on the other, it can be proud of its suffering. BUT–in either case–WHERE IS THE CROSS? The believing theologian may live in a manner which is congruent with the scriptures as he sees them, or the lay person may point to his life of sacrificial service, BUT WHERE IS THE CROSS?

Absent the teaching of the Cross, much that transpires within and without Christianity may appear to be consistent with the tenets of scripture. Much of the false teaching which abounds in this country would be stripped of its power to deceive if believers were grounded in the experiential understanding of the Cross. As the New Age comes of age, it will have swept increasing numbers of believers along with rhetoric that sounds like it accords with scripture–"Having a form of godliness, but denying the power thereof: from such turn away." (2 Tim. 2:5)

It is not my intention to de-emphasize any scriptural injunction such as evangelism, discipleship, prayer, and instruction in the scriptures but, rather, to point out that the understanding and experience of the Cross is not optional–it is a command: "Likewise reckon ye also yourselves to be dead indeed unto sin, but alive unto God through Jesus Christ our Lord. Neither yield ye your members as instruments of unrighteousness unto sin: but yield yourselves unto God, as those that are alive from the dead and your members as instruments of righteousness unto God." (Rom. 6:11,13) None of the disciplines of the Christian life is to be ignored, but each is to be practiced in the power of the Holy Spirit–not in the strength of the flesh. Without the reality of the Cross, the disciplines of the Christian life will result in the flesh becoming stronger and increasingly resistant to meddling questions such as, BUT WHERE IS THE CROSS?

Why has the church forsaken its heritage and traded its birthright for a mess? When it comes to the cure of souls with emotional, mental, and behavioral symptoms, many churches have all but gone out of business.

Prior to mid-century, Bible-believing, fundamental churches held suspect all forms of psychology and psychiatry. After that time there appeared men on the scene such as Dr. Clyde Narramore who began to popularize an approach called 'Christian psychology'. A moment's reflection will reveal that this is a contradiction in terms; by definition, psychology is secular since it is a study of the *psyche*–not the spirit of man. The addition of a scriptural veneer, however thick, does nothing to alter the fact that the core of psychology is secular or humanistic. Though psychology gives us some understanding of the thoughts, feelings and behavior of man, the therapeutic application of its tenets to change man is but to treat the symptoms and exacerbate the problem which is consummate selfishness.

As Christian educational institutions rushed to embrace this 'new kid on the block', ministerial students were taught systematically to refer believers with soul (psychological) difficulties for 'professional' help. Gradually, the seminaries began to employ psychologists and psychiatrists to teach students. Thus, the cycle was complete when those schooled in the world's methods began to peddle their wares to the leadership of the church. It is the author's opinion that much of the liberalism which pervades a number of the seminaries in this country rode into the seminary on the back of psychology.

As I have questioned those who earned the Master of Divinity degree from seminaries regarding the number of counseling courses required for the degree, the answer is usually, "One" or sometimes, a grand sum total of "Two". If the pastor has not had sufficient training to feel comfortable ministering one-on-one, why would he believe his lay people could be used of God in such a way?

After the referral mentality was thoroughly entrenched by the 60's with the participation of the seminaries, they began to offer master's degrees in counseling–most of which were patterned after 'Christian' psychology. In other words, after they had parceled out most of the market to the behavioral sciences, they began to market a product! By this time, so many believers had been referred to the world for an answer that few turned to the church; they had been thoroughly convinced by the Christian establishment that they needed 'professional' help. At this writing, some seminaries are turning out more counselors than pastors which is a sad commentary on the power of the preaching of the Cross to change lives. They are properly reading the future in that one-on-one ministry will be the greatest need of the church in the 90's; however, *it should be done by all of the members of the body–not just a select few with 'professional' training.* If this is to be done, it will be necessary that the Holy Spirit be the One who is doing the work through yielded believers; otherwise, help will not be available to the rank and file believer once the 'professional's' appointment book is full.

If the theology taught by a seminary is powerful enough to change lives from the pulpit, why should there not be a one-to-one correspondence between that which is taught in the pulpit and that which is inculcated in the counseling room? This author has known of a number of churches over the years where that which was done in counseling was in direct contradiction to the Biblical message from the pulpit and, sometimes, over the airwaves. In fact, one seminary professor told his counseling students that what they learned in theology would have no bearing on their counseling studies.

Why should this be? The author has tried on numerous occasions to enter into dialogue with nationally known pastors, educators, and educational institutions. Despite the protestations of openness, it tends to be a closed system.

On two occasions, I attended major conferences of believers–one in St. Louis and one in Los Angeles. In both places I noted that the president of a major school of graduate education was sitting alone. I approached them with the opener that I would like to discuss what we were doing in Christian counseling. The response of both was identical: "You will have to talk with someone in our psychology or counseling department". Though one was a Th.D. and the other was a Ph.D., neither felt comfortable to discuss what I see to be a spiritual ministry. They saw it to be a professional specialty with which they were not sufficiently versed to dialogue without the support of their specialists in the area. Of course, discussing it with their psychology departments would have been a dead end since psychology and spiritual counseling are two different disciplines and "never the twain shall meet".

Seminaries have gained respectability by teaching that which is currently in vogue, and psychologists and psychiatrists have churches as their greatest network of referrals. The turf has been neatly divided such that the church deals with the 'minor issues' or spiritual problems (translated as sin issues) and the 'professionals' deal with the psychological symptoms and are usually rewarded well for their ministrations. However, the great reduction in third party payments (insurance) is likely to make those professions much less lucrative than in the heyday of the past quarter century. Even so, many seminary students are assiduously working toward degrees that will qualify them to receive such third party payments from a well that is rapidly going dry.

Insurance companies and employers are taking drastic measures to reduce the amount of funds expended for alcohol and substance abuse and for extended periods of treatment of that which is commonly diagnosed as psychiatric illness. This is not to say that there is no such thing as organic brain problems; but it is my considered opinion, tempered by more than two decades of experience, that such problems are a small percentage of those treated in the offices of psychotherapists and in the psychiatric wards of hospitals. Until recently, about one third of the beds in hospitals in the country have been occupied by 'psychiatric' patients; and the cost to the hospital for those patients is a fraction of that billed for general hospital patients. Just as many restaurants cover their overhead with the revenue from alcohol, hospitals have made good revenue from the same customers! *The insurance companies have decided that the 'gravy train' will have a much tighter schedule from here on!* In Denver, a hospital has recently closed its doors after many years because of the tightening of third party payments and its dependence upon income from substance abuse programs which tended to be rather lucrative.

Just as the state mental hospitals have put mental patients on chemical straight jackets (medication) and dumped them into the streets (much of the homeless population), *those who have spent extended periods of time in various kinds of psychiatric treatment funded by insurance companies will be camping on the doorsteps of our churches.* What are we going to do with such an influx of people with some major emotional difficulties when most churches are all but impotent in dealing with the minor issues they have been accorded by the 'professionals'?

The churches (a conglomeration of people) will be saying (or groaning) along with many of their individual constituents, "We just do not know where to turn!" When the state and insurance companies quit bailing out the church, we may just be forced to get back to the first century way of doing things— *"For the preaching of the cross is to them that perish foolishness; but unto us which are saved it is the power of God"* (1 Cor. 1:18).

RESISTANCE TO CHANGE

Taking the position that the root problem underlying much, if not most, of the mental, emotional, and behavioral symptoms is ultimately spiritual has been far from popular; and more opposition has come from within the Christian establishment than from unbelievers. In both of my graduate degrees I received my greatest help from non-Christians but had to cope with the resistance of believers. The following points are some that detractors would cite in support of Christian psychology or in defense of the *status quo* in Christian counseling/discipleship.

THE NATURE OF THE BELIEVER

Most theologians and devotional writers of the last century have held the position that the lost man has one nature while the believer has two–the only creature on planet Earth to be saddled with such a problem! The word, *nature,* is a great part of the problem when it is confused with the old man and new man–old nature/new nature. The flesh with its propensity to sin (sometimes described as a nature) is not seen as separate and distinct from the old man. Our relationship with Adam through the old man is not seen as having been severed when we are "baptized into Christ" (Rom. 6:3). The result is that the believer is tacitly held to be *in Adam* and *in Christ,* simultaneously. Some of those holding a two nature position would allow this to prevent their giving a thorough evaluation to the entire counseling/ discipleship approach. Some would also infer a teaching of sinless perfection, holding that all sin emanates from the sin nature even though the scripture clearly states that the *flesh* is the believer's problem (Galatians 5:16,17). Though sinless perfection has never been my position, there have been those who have made this groundless assertion over the years. Have you ever noticed that people are usually *down* on what they are not *up* on?

THE MODEL OF MAN AND TERMINOLOGY

Some of those adhering to a two-part or dichotomous model of man find great difficulty in considering an approach based on a three-part or trichotomous model of man. There is ample scriptural warrant for trichotomy in I Thes. 5:23 and Hebrews 4:12 and many other places where trichotomy may be inferred, though it is not stated definitively. Since those holding to dichotomy are in the majority, this position is relegated to the minority opinion; some would hold that only the naive or uninformed continue in the position of trichotomy. Some interpretations of scripture which are based on the trichotomous view, would not fit into dichotomous thinking. For example, there is nothing in the dichotomous view to be crucified. If you crucify the soul, only the body or a vegetable remains; if the body is crucified, there is very little left behind! The lack of functional definition of terms, whether applied to a dichotomous or trichotomous model, has added to the confusion. Attempting concise definitions, where broad or overlapping definitions have been generally accepted, draws fire from some quarters.

The multichotomous view of man is finding acceptance in some theological circles–the model of man is expanded to as many parts as one chooses to give it. However, some of those who are generous in assigning a variety of parts would not allow the spirit, being one of those parts, to be a separate functioning entity. In other words, they become rather narrow minded at this juncture!

Departing from the more commonly accepted norm of dichotomy is, at the best, unpopular with those who are accorded the privilege of molding public opinion from their ivory towers.

OBJECTIONS FROM THEOLOGY

Various systems of theology have been devised by man in an effort to understand and harmonize the scriptures. Being man-made, all have some truth and some error. However, adherents to a particular theological system have a tendency to force everything to fit the system.

Some would hold that co-crucifixion is a positional or forensic truth which can not become an experiential reality in the life of the believer. Obviously, such a person could not accept an approach which holds this as central and pivotal to a Spirit-filled or Christ-centered life. Brokenness is not a popular concept, and only those who have undergone the brokenness of the Cross have experienced the power of the resurrection. This is not to say that they have arrived, except at the bottom; and this is hardly something of which to boast! When a person has based not only his life but also his professional reputation on a contrary theological position which excludes the experienced Cross, he is unlikely to give serious consideration to a system of teaching which he regards as error at best and heresy at worst.

THE ENCROACHMENTS OF PSYCHOLOGY

In the last three decades the church at large has accepted the tenets of psychology, with various scriptural overlays, as the method of choice in dealing with the problems of the soul. Psychology has, in fact, become the handmaiden to the church.

It frequently escapes notice that the various schools of psychology are rooted in atheistic presuppositions. Veneering with scripture does not change the core; when the core is fleshly, the results of therapy utilizing the approach will be, also.

However, that which has been learned by the behavioral sciences, which does not disagree with scripture, can be used to good advantage for the purpose of understanding only. It is when it is used for treatment or therapy that it becomes a substitute for the work of the Holy Spirit.

OBJECTIONS FROM EXPERIENCE
(Or, lack of experience)

Those who have not undergone brokenness and who have not experienced the Cross can not appreciate or really understand, spiritually, a counseling approach which makes this central. It makes no difference whether their theology is identical or hostile if the experience of the Cross in the life is not a reality. Only thus can one know the power of the Cross to transform his life and the lives of others. The experiential aspect is fully covered in my first book, *Handbook to Happiness*.

Absent the reality of the Cross in the life, one would necessarily embrace an approach to helping people where this was not a requirement. Some of these would hold to theology which accommodates identification with Christ in death and resurrection and, at the same time, practice that which negates it.

INCONSISTENCY IN THOUGHT AND THEOLOGICAL POSITION

There are those who are trichotomous by conviction whose thinking is more in line with a dichotomous model. That is to say that functions of the spirit are attributed to the soul and vice-versa. Such inconsistency causes one to arrive at erroneous conclusions. The humanistic bias which deprives man of a truly spiritual dimension has its fallout in the thinking of believers. Identity and meaning become interwoven with the soul or personality rather than the spirit. A person's essential identity derives from his family of origin. The sinner's family of origin is Adam; the believer's family of origin is Christ. We are in one or the other, but not in both simultaneously!

Then, there are those who hold to dichotomy who walk in the Spirit and are greatly used of God and who, by definition, have experienced the Cross. This, in my opinion, is inconsistent with their avowed theology in that there is nothing to be crucified in the dichotomous model of man.

If there is no Adamic life (or spirit) to be crucified, the soul must continually be improved upon as taught in an incomplete view of progressive sanctification. In my opinion, this position logically eventuates in works, or law, instead of grace; whereas the trichotomous position is more supportive of co-crucifixion and grace. Confusion of terms, differing theological positions and the encroachments of humanistic thinking have obscured the centrality of the Cross in thought and, thus, blinded many believers to their true identity in Christ.

MISINFORMATION

Those who do not understand and/or are in disagreement with the approach have made inferences which they have disseminated as truth. Their reputations as authority figures have caused those who want to find fault with our approach to use them to prove their case.

For example, Dr. Bruce Narramore implied in one of his books (*You are Someone Special*, p. 106) that I teach the annihilation of the personality (or the Freudian term, ego, as he puts it) which is not true; on page 105, he stooped to the level of ridicule. In the remainder of the chapter, he betrays his inadequate understanding of the believers' identification with Christ.

Dr. Jay Adams wrote and has stated in lectures that I hold (or would not deny) that the believer atones for his own sin (*More Than Redemption*, 1978, Eerdmans) but has since toned it down in a later edition of the book (*More Than Redemption*, Zondervan) after I confronted him by letter over his groundless assertion.

Dr. Martin Bobgan in his recent self-published book, *Psychoheresy* pp. 95,96, found fault with my model and left the impression that I teach heresy simply by being included in a book with such a title. Although I refuted his allegation that I teach rejection as the reason a believer must experience the work of the Cross in his life in the presence of David Hunt, face to face, he still saw fit to attempt to undermine the ministry of GFI.

I believe God calls us as His ambassadors to be more accurate in our scholarship and more loving than the foregoing mentions from these brothers represent. My purpose in pointing out these three inaccurate representations is not to seek personal redress from these brethren but, rather, to restore GFI's credibility with those leaders who have been misled by them.

It is not uncommon for professors in seminaries to indoctrinate their students with inferences they have made about our approach. The result is that students tend to accept the inferences as truth rather than doing an independent investigation–such a unique approach as talking to the author or, as a minimum, reading his books and allowing him to speak for himself. Though the intent may not be malicious, a misrepresentation based on an inference has been propagated as truth in all too many instances.

DUALITY IN THINKING–*The bifurcation between counseling as ministry and counseling as behavioral science.*

Since the institutions for Christian education, for the most part, have not taught a distinctively spiritual approach to counseling which can be practiced by all students, the inference on the part of the student (if not the administration) is that counseling is a specialty requiring thorough schooling in the behavioral sciences. Thus, it is not uncommon to hear a person holding a Doctor of Theology degree say, "I'm not a counselor", when faced with a believer who has soul (personality) problems which may, in fact, be a derivative of deep-seated spiritual needs.

It is the rule, rather than the exception, that a

seminary does not make a one-to-one correspondence between that which is taught in theology and that which is taught in counseling. Because of the duality in thinking, they do not recognize an inherent contradiction in their approach to helping people with problems. It is not at all uncommon to find that which is taught in counseling classes to be in utter contradiction to that which is taught in theology.

All too frequently, the ministerial student graduates with answers for the lost and referrals for the saved! As previously stated, the seminary student who doesn't major in counseling is required to take one or two courses which would hardly be sufficient to develop confidence in such a role. Thus, it is not mysterious as to why many pastors feel inadequate when faced with severely disturbed people. However, his training allows him to refer such persons without guilt since this is a 'psychological' problem to be treated by another discipline–psychology or psychiatry–the humanistic presuppositions of these disciplines notwithstanding.

THE SECULAR MODEL
IN CHRISTIAN EDUCATION

Humanistic educators have decided that helping people is a function of graduate education. Therefore, counseling courses are taught, almost exclusively, at the graduate level. Following this model, there has been little or no teaching of counseling courses at the undergraduate level in many Bible colleges. Most seminaries, even though graduate level, do little in training *all* ministerial students to work with emotional disturbances since this is seen as a 'specialty'. The secular model indicates a secular answer, and the Christian institutions for higher education have imbibed in more of this than they would care to admit. The rationale frequently given is appealing to 'common grace' or 'all truth is God's truth' which is supposed to give sanction to teaching approaches to counseling which do not rely upon the Holy Spirit to transform lives.

This willing truce enables the theological and psychological communities to map out the turf to the satisfaction of both, while leaving many believers with only partial answers that may provide some temporary symptomatic relief.

A SUGGESTED MODEL FOR EDUCATION AND MINISTRY

Since there is a spiritual answer for soul problems (non-organic), it is the believer who should be discipled and trained to work with them. The training should be made available in the local church as well as in the Bible college and seminary. Those whose spiritual gift involves working with people on a one-on-one basis can be trained without the benefit of formal education, except in extreme cases.

Spiritual counseling should be the assiduous application of scripture in the power of the Spirit to the soul problems of believers. As such, it is not the domain of the academician but of the spiritual believer called of God and gifted for such a ministry. This topic is further developed in Chapter 6.

Those who have experienced the Cross can teach it from the pulpit or in the classroom (Sunday school, Bible school or seminary) or at the kitchen table and let God receive the glory for transforming lives.

INDIVIDUAL AND CORPORATE IDENTITY

When the identity is based on the soul and those desires which will satisfy it, nothing permanently satisfies–*enough is never enough*; and there is always the quest for something to take its place. When the church does not base its identity on Christ, it must continue to capitalize on those things that have gained the attention of its members if it is going to attract them and involve them in its programs. The world has yet to mimic the Cross in its quest for identity since the Cross speaks of self sacrifice–not self enhancement. Only when the believer has sacrificed himself at the Cross will he be attracted to a church which not only encourages sacrifice but demands it. Without such sacrifice, there is really no commitment to Christ or to His body. Lack of commitment is a central issue in declining church attendance and the church hopping that is epidemic today.

Churches are generally united when they are involved in a project or a fight. Usually, the project must be of a tangible nature such that any believer may become involved, regardless of his spirituality, or lack thereof. Building programs can involve everyone, even though there may be fights interspersed over the color of the carpet and other major issues which will lose their significance with the passing of time or the razing of the building. Many of the issues of eternal significance go begging while carnal believers hassle over temporal issues that divide and destroy.

It is equally easy to get believers to unite to fight, particularly when the issue is one that involves matters related to the soul, since all can understand and have a piece of the action. Spiritual issues tend to have fewer adherents since they may not be understood, and sacrifice may be that which is required. If the spiritual issue does not impact his own identity, it is likely that the average believer will depend upon the pastor or others to stand in the gap while he busies himself with more pressing matters.

In most churches' way of doing things, *Christian is not who we* are; *it is what we* do. We *do* lunch, and we *do* church; and, frequently, one form of food lasts about as long as the other! As individual identities change, with their interests based on their identities, the church changes to accommodate the fads and fashions. Since the church is not anchored in its identity in Christ, neither are the people who comprise the church. The Christian must be able to commit to the church because it is committed to the Lordship of Christ. When the values of the church change along with society, there is nothing stable upon which a person can anchor his personal and family life.

In a very real way, we can say that the church has lost its soul since, in all too many instances, the soul or personality of the church does not manifest consistent empowering of the Holy Spirit. The soul in the individual should be the expression of his spirit. When he lives out of his soul instead of his spirit, then there is a conflict between what he *is* and what he *does*. The Word clearly shows this as a conflict between the flesh (a carnal condition of the soul or personality) and the Spirit (Gal. 5:17). When the majority of the believers are living out of their souls rather than their spirits, the reflection of their collective souls in the Body will be a lifeless church or one that has, in effect, lost its soul–its ability to reflect and minister the Spirit of the Living God.

In past times, the church was the center of family life and social life. We might say that, to a great extent, there was a Christian culture. Today, we have a pagan culture where Christian values are decried rather than esteemed. Indeed, the Biblical viewpoint is considered antiquated and irrelevant because there are no absolutes in our present culture. Humanistic decisions no longer take into consideration whether something is right or wrong based on God's revealed Word. Issues such as abortion and homosexuality, which are clearly in violation of both the spirit and the letter of the law, are treated as civil issues which have to do with man and his choices rather than conforming to God's clear commands.

When our country was founded, we had one nation under God; now, we have a fragmented nation under humanism. The fragmentation has come as a result of our letting down the spiritual barriers in the church such that it is no longer the conscience of the nation as it was in the early days of this country. Only as we get back to basics as individuals, families and churches will there be sufficient transformations where the church will again be what God intended it to be–a living organism with the resurrection life of the Lord Jesus Christ to replace the deadness of programs which are all too often carried out in the strength of the flesh. To a great degree, the church has lost its identity and its sense of mission to confront the world system, largely since it has drawn so much from secular sources and has come to depend upon the arm of the flesh in more ways than it is comfortable to admit. Having defaulted on its power Source, it is greatly in need of revival if it is once again to become a major force within society. That being the case, there have been numerous strategies employed to return the church to her former glory; however, many, if not most, of these have not made the Cross central to their message, methods, and goals. Therefore, they have not resulted in widespread revival though many have been greatly used of God. We will consider these in the next chapter as we survey the multitudinous ways in which individuals and groups have attempted to bring new life to the church.

N. Balkanski

CHAPTER IV
ATTEMPTS TO RESUSCITATE
THE CHURCH

In the last half century, there has been a constant stream of individuals and movements which have been used of God as corrective measures in various aspects of His sagging church. It is my premise that many of these have been ordained of God to accomplish that which would not have been needed if the church had been functioning as He intended. He *will* get His work done even if He has to resort to Plan B, parachurch organizations, to accomplish it! I believe that most of the movements discussed below were necessary to pick up the slack where the church was not meeting the particular need. Some of them were corrective measures in the church in an attempt to get it back to where it had been in years past; few of them brought the preaching of the Cross, as we are emphasizing it here, into their teaching as a central focus.

Therefore, just as with the Reformation, some aspects of the church's failures were remedied only to leave a void that would require another different, if not better, alternative to that which was presently being taught by the church in its varied manifestations. It is not my purpose to condemn the efforts of the individuals and groups which is evidenced by the fact that the organization I founded and my own personal ministry is included in the roster of movements discussed–one which would have been unnecessary if the church had not departed from a clear emphasis on the teaching of the Cross from the pulpit and in the personal ministry of believers.

FUNDAMENTALISM

One of the early movements, *World Baptists*, which has had a noticeable impact on the face of Christianity in this country was inaugurated by Rev. J. Frank Norris who endeavored to get the church back to teaching the fundamentals of the faith. His work was primarily centered in the South where he built a Bible college and seminary (Ft. Worth, TX). After a while, there was a branching off from his work in the form of Baptist Bible Fellowship. Out of this movement there developed a missions organization that has sent missionaries literally around the world. They have started several Bible colleges and have had a great ministry in emphasizing the inerrancy of the Scriptures and in evangelism. Many of the major churches in this country have their roots in this movement. Also, Bob Jones was instrumental in founding a movement and a school which has been a bastion of fundamentalism. (Incidentally, I regard myself as a fundamentalist; so I am not using this term in a pejorative sense.)

The major emphasis has been evangelism, church planting and missions. In so doing, there has not been an equal thrust in discipleship, when discipleship is defined as having taken up the Cross in experience according to Luke 14:27: "And whosoever doth not bear his cross, and come after me, cannot be my disciple".

SUPER AGGRESSIVE EVANGELISM

This movement, as the name implies, put such an emphasis on evangelism that it eclipsed most other ministries in the church. It resulted in the building of some major churches, some of which could be termed 'balloon ministries'. When the pastor who had been the guiding light in the formation and building of the church passed from the scene, the church tended to decline just about as rapidly as it had been built, much as a balloon tends to deflate very rapidly when it is punctured. Some of these recovered, but many never returned to be the force in evangelism that they once had been.

REVIVALISM

Many fundamental and evangelical churches have had a history of scheduling 'revivals' once or twice a year. It is not uncommon to hear a Baptist pastor tell someone, "I will be going to a certain place to preach a revival". Usually, he is referring to evangelistic meetings which have come to be known by that name. In many churches, this is a device to 'pump up' the members and get them sort of recharged for another year (or, at least, a week or two!). The revivalist is able to say some things the pastor wants to, and needs to, but is fearful of the reaction if he does. If the ire of the flesh of the congregation is exposed, the visiting revivalist may safely duck out after the 'revival' is over; and the pastor can place the blame elsewhere and get back to placating the flesh. You see, if revival had truly taken place, the flesh would have been dealt a crippling blow; and many of the soul ills would have been healed in the process. How many revivalists actually preach the *message of revival, the crucified life*?

Could this not be the reason why true revival seldom accompanies the ministry of one who is called to 'preach a revival'?

EVANGELISTIC CRUSADES

In this century, various evangelists have come on the scene who have been greatly used of God. One has only to think back to D. L. Moody, Billy Sunday, Billy Graham, Luis Palau and a host of lesser lights to realize that many believers still living today owe the fact that they heard the gospel in a way that resulted in their salvation to one of these men or someone who was directly or indirectly influenced by their ministries.

D. L. Moody ministered in crusades for several years before the truth we are treating here was a reality in his own life. When I met Luis Palau in Switzerland in 1974, he told me that Galatians 2:20 was his life verse. Though I have never heard him speak, I have read some of his writing where he clearly teaches the truth of our co-death and co-resurrection with Christ. In my opinion, he stands out in bold relief when compared with the ministry that we associate with the average evangelist.

As you think back on the evangelistic messages you have heard from any evangelist or pastor, how frequently did you hear both aspects of the Cross clearly taught? Of course, a sinner must have a faithful presentation of Christ's sacrificial work at Calvary if he is to be convicted of sin and regenerated. He must know that the Blood of the Lord Jesus paid the penalty for his sins that he may be forgiven; however, is it not equally important to instruct him about his new life? Yes, he must see that the *Blood is for his sins*; but he must know that the *Cross is for the sinner* if he is to walk in the new life in the power of the Spirit.

By all means, we should continue evangelistic crusades; but why limit the gospel to the forgiveness of sins when the new believer can be instructed in the walk in the Spirit through the experienced Cross at the same time? This omission in evangelism has much to do with the spiritual anemia suffered by the average church in this country today. May God forgive us for such an incomplete presentation of the gospel!

HYPE OR PERSONALITIES

Who has not seen the parade of well known personalities giving testimony to having been saved? These are heard in major evangelistic crusades, in the pulpits of large churches, and on television presentations. Occasionally, these are people who have been recently saved or purport to have been. Some, such as Chuck Colson, go on with the Lord to be used in mighty ways; others, who were not truly born again or who were mere babes in Christ, have later made a mockery of that which they once held to be the most important happening in their lives.

One can not deny the influence well known individuals can have on the lives of the listeners. For example, a friend of mine who recently went to be with the Lord, Jim Irwin, made great use of the public recognition of his name as an astronaut and Moon walker to gain a hearing for the gospel. However, he took the time to build a track record and mature as a believer before he began publicly to proclaim the gospel to the watching world.

I believe we do a disservice to such people by putting them in the limelight before they have had opportunity to mature in the shadows. For example, a physician who is born again instantly becomes a minor prophet in the eyes of many, even though the physician knows that

137

(s)he is yet a mere babe in Christ. Being thrust into a position of prominence in the church denies such a person the needed time to go through the necessary stages of growth, most of which do not happen over night!

All of us know of some who have been thrust into national prominence without sufficient maturity who have fallen by the wayside in sin or unbelief. I do not fault them as much as those who may have had some selfish motives in presenting them to the church and to the world prematurely as a trophy of grace. Doesn't the scripture state that we are to "lay hands suddenly on no man"? (1 Tim. 5:22)

CHARISMATIC RENEWAL MOVEMENT

For the last three decades, the charismatic renewal movement in its many manifestations has become an increasingly strong force within the church. In the beginning, it branched off of the Pentecostal movement which had its roots around the turn of the century in this country.

There have been various and sundry personalities who began churches and movements in an attempt to bring new life to the church. Some of these have matured into stable churches, or movements within a variety of churches, while others have run their course and have faded from the scene. The prominence given to the gifts of the Spirit, primarily healing and deliverance, has resulted in the rise of a number of major ministries in this and other countries. Also, there have been major movements within mainline denominations, including some of the more liturgical ones, which have made a significant impact on the members and, sometimes, the leaders of those movements.

It has been my experience that many of these movements have deepened their roots in the scripture compared with my first introduction to them in the 70's. Many have gone from a more experience-centered, but doctrinally shallow, stance to develop leaders who are being greatly used of God as Bible teachers.

The Discipleship or Shepherding movement was one that grew out of the general charismatic grouping. In the last two or three years, the leadership of that movement has publicly acknowledged some of the excesses and deficiencies that characterized the movement. Thus, as with so many movements, it was necessary to make some 'mid-course' corrections; but there were a number of people hurt in the process.

Out of the Jesus movement of the 60's Chuck Smith began Calvary Chapel and proceeded to establish others in various parts of the country. Then, John Wimber branched out from this original grouping and started the Vineyard movement which has a large number of adherents in this country and England.

PROGRAMITIS

During my tenure in the church, there has been the tendency to replace one program with another in a vain attempt to find something that works. Once the programs were duly installed, God was asked to bless the latest revised version of the last revision. Most of the programs were devised by the ingenuity of man, and many had excellent features which met perceived needs of the group or groups involved.

The problem is not that a program is developed but that it was not born in the heart of God for that particular part of His Body. This being the case, He was under no obligation to bless and prosper it.

If we hearken back to the third chapter under the heading, *But Where is the Cross?*, I think we can conclude that the Cross is not central in much of the programming devised by the church or by groups marketing materials to the church. In fact, as was pointed out, most of the materials are strangely silent on the subject, which accounts for some of the lack of understanding of this crucial message by the average church member.

Programs called into being by the Holy Spirit will enjoy His blessing and will result in changed (or *exchanged* lives); those which are not put Him under no such obligation. Someone has said that "Man proposes, but God disposes". Would that we would wait on Him to provide the direction and witness the empowering by the Holy Spirit of that which He has called into being! A book that is excellent regarding the abundant life and which puts dependence upon programs into proper perspective is *Faith is the Victory* written by a pastor in the 50's, Buell Kazee (Eerdmans and Tyndale House).

CONFERENCES, SEMINARS, WORKSHOPS, ETC.

Since almost all of the aspects of the church have gone begging in some particulars, there has been the need for the vacuum to be filled. I will mention some of these without going into detail as most are well known to those who are active in church circles. All of them have strong points which commend them to some segment of the church; and, being implemented by mortal man, all have deficiencies which would benefit by correction.

The order of listing them will not necessarily be in a chronological sequence nor in their order of importance. However, it will be noted that there tends to be a trend which runs its course; and, then, another takes its place. For example, *Evangelism Explosion* under the direction of Dr. James Kennedy was a major player in the late 60's and 70's and continues to be used of God until this writing.

There was a time when almost everyone was into finding his spiritual gifts and attempting to make maximum use of them in the Body. Campus Crusade for Christ has been greatly used of God in evangelism in various parts of the world and continues to fulfill the Great Commission at this writing; God has used this organization in the Eastern Block in Europe and Russia in ways that defy estimation.

Church Growth seminars and consultation have been extremely popular in recent years. Piggy-backing on them has been the current emphasis on marketing with a flood of books of late being written in this area.

With the advent of television we have the bane or blessing, depending upon the viewpoint, of the Electronic Church. Recent developments concerning central figures in televangelism have done much to bring reproach upon God's work, not only in this country, but in other countries where such figures have been prominent. On the positive side, Dr. Charles Stanley through *In Touch Ministries* has been at the forefront of declaring the message of the Cross; I encounter believers all across the country that depend upon his ministry for spiritual growth from week to week since they are not exposed to this emphasis in their own churches.

Family life centers have been built at great expense by some churches which concern themselves with body building in addition to the building up of the Body. I visited one such center in one of the major churches in the country and was impressed by the quality of the equipment available to the constituents.

I asked my guide, "How much does membership in this church cost?". Though there is nothing wrong with providing such facilities, it is possible that there could be a use for such funds that would be a greater investment in the kingdom of God.

There are seminars available on almost all aspects of church life, and parachurch organizations have been greatly used of God in meeting this need. All of these have been developed by believers who are members of churches; but all that are truly of God could, and should, have been carried out by the church. However, now that the void has been filled by individual ministries and/or parachurch organizations, many could be phased out if the church would return to doing what it never should have ceased to do. In this regard, I think particularly of Grace Fellowship International which God called me to found in 1969. If enough churches of various denominations would pick up the training and equip their people, there would be no reason for the continued existence of GFI. The same would be true of many of the other organizations which are concerned about various areas of deficiency into which they have been drawn by the Spirit of God–assuming that they truly are valid ministries.

MEGA CHURCHES

This is the current rage with pastors making pilgrimages to Korea and to points within the United States to observe the phenomena which is held up to be the success story for other pastors to emulate. This is not to say that God is not using mega churches to touch lives for the Lord Jesus Christ; however, would the attraction be as great if the invitation were openly stated, "Come here, and lose your life!"? I have noted in more than two decades of ministry that believers are not exactly standing in long lines to take advantage of such an invitation. In fact, even when they come for counseling on their own initiative, it is a sobering thought that they must lose control to Another.

I am not a prophet nor the son of a prophet, but it strikes me that building expansive (and expensive) churches in a shrinking economy may soon reach the point of diminishing returns. If the time comes that people can no longer drive the inordinate distances to church or that they see the need for home churches or smaller churches within their own communities, the commodious structures with the attendant debt-servicing could become a major problem and poor testimony across the country. Mortgage companies will find it difficult to find another use for single-use facilities if they are forced to foreclose on them. After I began this writing, a major church in Oklahoma has filed for bankruptcy because of the inordinate debt.

OTHER AREAS AND ORGANIZATIONS ARE:

Christian psychology, Deeper Life Conferences, Discipleship, Marriage and Family, Fathers' seminars, Money Management, Counseling seminars and workshops, Prayer seminars, Divorce Issues, Music Seminars, Pastors' seminars, Women's Seminars, Deliverance Ministries, Inner Healing, Bible Study Fellowship, Precept Ministries, The Navigators, InterVarsity Fellowship, Institute in Basic Youth Conflicts, World Vision, Samaritan's Purse, Marriage Encounter, Keswick teaching, etc, etc. The list is seemingly endless, and many lives have been touched and transformed by the Spirit of God with world leaders having been raised up in the ranks of many of these ministries.

The point is not whether they have accomplished a

purpose, even God's purpose; but why were they necessary in the first place? If the church had been fulfilling its God-ordained purpose, there would not have been the fertile ground, or vacuum, which caused many of these ministries to be called into being by God. And what can we do as members of the Body of Christ to get back to the place that the local expressions are vibrant, Spirit-filled bodies such that God's Hand is directing and empowering? I would like to propose a novel idea that death is the only way out! It is absolutely amazing the things that death will cure! This is because the death of which we are speaking is always accompanied by resurrection (Romans 6:3-6). Let's look in the next chapter at the similarity between God's dealing with the individual believer and His dealing with the corporate body–the church. In my opinion, both must come to the end of themselves if they are to minister in resurrection power and true revival is to be continuous.

CHAPTER V
LIFE OUT OF DEATH
The Scriptural Way of Revival

TAKE OFF THE LIFE SUPPORT SYSTEMS!

Many families are faced with the dilemma of artificially prolonging the lives of their loved ones; or, if such extraordinary methods have not been employed, should it be done? When is the right time to remove the life supports and let death that is inevitable come naturally? These are difficult questions to face, and all of us trust that we will never be put in that position.

In the previous chapter, we have looked at many good things that are being done that could be construed to be ministering life to the church from without. Credit was given where credit was due in that many of these individuals and movements have been greatly blessed of the Lord in reaching the lost for Christ and, in some cases, bringing revival to those who were defeated and hurting. The question that comes is whether in so doing, are we crutching the church and making it dependent on outside resources? *Should we continue to do this, or should we see if God is capable of giving life to His own Body?* I believe that the resurrection of the Lord Jesus Christ from the dead answered this question adequately and for all time.

Revival is the term generally given to the ministrations involving one who has had a close brush with death; we say that he has been revived. Similarly, the church has had life–the life of the Lord Jesus Christ; and the embers that are there need to be fanned by the wind of the Holy Spirit into full flame. The life is there, but the expression of it leaves much to be desired in all too many cases.

Our conception of revival will have much to do with the manner in which we pray for it and the expectation that we have regarding the answer to such prayer and, indeed, recognizing revival when God does send it. I have heard believers debate as to whether there will be another revival before our Lord's return; there are sincere believers who take both sides of this discussion.

I think most of us picture revival as the sovereign moving of the Holy Spirit in answer to believing prayer, repentance and obedience such that whole churches, cities, states or nations are radically affected. In such a revival, believers would get right with each other and a host of lost people would be born into the Kingdom of God. History is replete with this having happened at various times and places, and many books have been written on the great revivals of the last few centuries. I think particularly of Leonard Ravenhill, Roy Hession, J. Edwin Orr (who is now with the Lord), and of Dr. Richard Lovelace. All of these have been students of revival who have written and ministered in this vital area.

I would like to suggest that Romans 12:2 gives us a good definition of revival: "And be not conformed to this world: but be ye transformed by the renewing of your mind, that ye may prove what is that good, and acceptable, and perfect, will of God". And, indeed, this has taken place in all of the major revivals the world has known. However, is it necessary that revival follow these same patterns; or is it that we must meet the same conditions? We know that God has not changed and that it is His will for us to be conformed to His image (Romans 8:29). Therefore, it can not be God who is holding up revival–either individually or corporately; to hold to such a stratagem would be to depict God as being capricious with His children. God forbid that we should hold such a view! Since that could never be the case, should we not be about the task of determining what our role is in facilitating revival? I am not saying that we can manipulate God; but, rather, when we meet the conditions that He has clearly laid down, He will fulfill His promise.

It is strange how we apply one set of criteria to the lost and a completely different set to the saved, as though God loves sinners more than He loves saints! Or, perhaps, we have more faith to believe that He will honor His Word and save the lost than that He will honor His Word to transform the lives of His children. We go out and witness to the lost and expect that the Holy Spirit will save those who have been prepared of the Spirit and are ready to turn to Him in faith and repentance, and He does! In other words, we declare the message of salvation to the lost and are not surprised when God saves them, and His Word does not return void.

However, when it comes to the saved who are defeated or, perhaps, living in sin and with great emotional pain, do we declare to them the clear message of revival and believe God to do exceeding abundantly above all that we can ask or think in the lives of those who have been prepared of the Spirit (Eph. 3:20)? Or, do we sigh and blame our lack of spiritual power on the 'end times' and reminisce about the 'good old days' when God sent revival upon His people?

I, for one, would like to stand up and be counted as

affirming that God is in the business of bringing revival into the lives of believers on a regular basis–here and now! The problem is not that God is capricious or that he withholds revival because of some dispensational problem that has been devised by man; the problem is that, in all too many cases, *we have ceased to preach revival due to our own unbelief and/or ignorance.* Or, to put it another way, we have quit preaching the Cross which has robbed much preaching of God's empowering: "For the preaching of the cross is to them that perish foolishness; but unto us which are saved it is the power of God" (I Cor. 1:18).

For more than two decades, we have seen God literally transform lives by renewing their minds as the Cross is proclaimed in its fullness in the counseling room. These are mostly believers who have suffered greatly due to the exigencies of life and, at times, due to their own sin. Some are lost and are presented with the claims of Christ regarding sin and repentance and Christ's sacrificial death for them, but they are also shown that their coming to Christ means losing their own life in exchange for His. Sins forgiven? Yes, but also a new life–the life of the Lord Jesus lived out in them.

Our problem is that we have preached the Cross for the lost but have, unwittingly, inculcated self-effort and/or therapy for the saved (Gal. 3:3) by not preaching the Cross to believers, which 1 Cor. 1:18 holds to be the power of God. Again, I come to the refrain, *But Where is the Cross*? When we do not clearly preach the *message* of revival, should we wonder that we do not witness the *results* of revival?

Many, if not most, of the attempts at resuscitation which were delineated in Chapter 4 do not make a clear emphasis on the Cross in the dimension of which we are now speaking. Should we be surprised, then, that the emphasis or current fad in Christian circles continues to change from year to year and that the emphasis that was all the rage a few years ago is now *passe'*? Or, to put it even more bluntly, should we wonder that excellent teaching, even that clearly based on scriptural principles, is not attended with transformed lives when it is done in the strength of the flesh? True resuscitation does not have life forced on the person from without, but the life within is revived and enabled to continue unabated.

Just as the lost person must be prepared and drawn by the Holy Spirit before the message of the gospel is to be efficacious, the believer to whom the message of the Cross is to be proclaimed must have been similarly prepared. He must be brought to the end of himself and trusting in the arm of the flesh if he is to be ready to submit himself to the work of the Cross in his life. This is amply described in *Handbook to Happiness*, Chapters 2 and 5. The resulting life transformation can best be described as revival or life out of death. With many believers there is a greater change when the Cross does its work than when the person was born again. When a person is saved but living out of fleshly resources, there remains many of the traits of the former life, particularly in the realm of psychological conflict and habit patterns. This same person may be radically transformed when he can say with Paul, "I am crucified with Christ: nevertheless I live; yet not I, but Christ liveth in me." (Gal. 2:20)

But what is the point I am trying to make? If an individual can experience this life transformation or revival as a result of the Holy Spirit's having prepared him for a presentation of the message of the Cross, why can't a church see the same thing on a larger scale? Could it not be that the message is not clearly and consistently taught or preached? It is my belief that a church must be brought to the end of itself, much in the same way that an individual believer is (see Diagram 2).

Since the average believer is living (or existing) and ministering in self effort, doesn't it follow that the average church, being made up of that type of believer, will be doing the same and seeing the same results–next to nothing? Yes, the believer may be able to reproduce himself and see the lost find new birth; but he has done just that–reproduced him*self*! And, the church reproduces itself in the lives of the believers entrusted to it and in those sent out to do various forms of ministry, whether locally or on the mission field.

Let's take a look at a depiction of the self-centered church which is parallel to that of the self-centered believer in Chapter 2 of *Handbook to Happiness*. Just as Christian psychology may be applied to the symptoms of the individual's personality rather than allowing the Holy Spirit to bring revival and transformation, various Christian approaches and emphases (resuscitation) are generally applied to the ailing life of the church; or, to put it in that vernacular, therapy is applied which may do wonders for the symptoms but never touch the problem–the self-life or fleshly approach to programming and ministry. Also, as in psychotherapy, if the symptoms get better, the problem is invariably worsened since the self-life (the problem) is strengthened in the process. However, everyone, or almost everyone (excluding the spiritually discerning), is encouraged as the wheels begin to turn again; but, all too frequently, it is the same old grind!

To continue the analogy of the treatment of a mental patient with psychotherapy and/or psychiatry, the patient may receive help and function much better than when being admitted. However, the patient rarely achieves a level of functioning which exceeds his best state prior to his 'breakdown'. When another episode occurs, some help is received; but, each time, he recovers to a level just slightly lower than the original recovery which means that the general trend is downward over a period of years. Just so, we have all seen churches, with the symptomatology listed in the diagram of the self-centered church, improve for a period of time only to go into a period of declension to be followed by another cycle until 'Ichabod' is all but written above its doors. . . .

If the 'patient' fails to respond to the infusion of life from without, it is deemed to be time to try a graft, with one pastor being cut off and another grafted into his place. It is well known that there are times when grafts do not 'take', and it is necessary to begin the process all over again—sometimes before complete healing has taken place. If the new pastor has not been through the death/resurrection process in his own life, he will not see the necessity for the entire church to go through it and will begin his own brand of resuscitation; on and on it goes, and where it stops nobody (except God) knows!

All of us are familiar with some churches which have gone through the above process for years; and, finally, the patient is officially declared dead, the doors closed, and the building sold to a struggling congregation, or to one which has outgrown its facilities, where the same process may begin all over again with different names and faces and their own unique approaches to resuscitation. . . .

However, there is a better way, even though it is admittedly radical; *death is the only way out*! The symptoms shown in the self-centered church must be brought to extinction as God brings the church to the end of itself. Most of the traits that we have described can be subsumed under the headings listed in the following diagram:

Diagram 1 The Self-Centered Church

In looking at the church, we will be referring to Paul's letter to the Ephesians which can be interpreted as being just as true of the corporate body of believers as it is of the individual. The reader may want to study Paul's other letters in this regard and glean different facets of the church to expand upon that which follows.

The *SPIRIT* in the diagram is being used to depict the true identity of the church as the organism that God ordained it to be. Just as with the individual, this identity or Spirit should be manifested to the watching world through the soul or visible manifestation of the church. This may be may be described as that which we are to be corporately–"every spiritual blessing" (Eph.1:3). This is delineated in Diagram 1 under similar headings to that of *Handbook to Happiness* for the individual believer:

1. SALVATION (or new birth) resulting in redemption and forgiveness; we, as a church, are a company of the redeemed (Eph.1:7): "In whom we have redemption through his blood, the forgiveness of sins, according to the riches of his grace."

2. ASSURANCE based on our sure inheritance (Eph.1:11,14): "In whom, also we have obtained an inheritance, being predestinated according to the purpose of him who worketh all things after the counsel of his own will: Which is is the earnest of our inheritance until the redemption of the purchased possession, unto the praise of his glory."

3. SECURITY based on our being sealed with the Spirit (Eph.1:13; 4:30): "In whom ye also trusted, after that ye heard the word of truth, the gospel of your salvation: in whom also after that ye believed, ye were sealed with that holy Spirit of promise."

4. ACCEPTANCE based on our being chosen (Eph.1:4) and adopted (Eph.1:5): "According as he hath chosen us in him before the foundation of the world, that we should be holy and without blame before him in love: Having predestinated us unto the adoption of children by Jesus Christ to himself, according to the good pleasure of his will."

5. IDENTITY IN A NEW FAMILY ("You", "We" and "Us"–Jew and Gentile) as described in Chapters 2 and 3, particularly in Eph. 2:13-19: "For through him we

both have access by one Spirit unto the Father. Now therefore ye are no more strangers and foreigners, but fellow citizens with the saints, and of the household of God." (Eph. 2:18,19)

6. POWER as described in Eph.1:18-20 and 3:20: "The eyes of your understanding being enlightened; that ye may know what is the hope of his calling, and what the riches of the glory of his inheritance in the saints, And what is the exceeding greatness of his power to us-ward who believe, according to the working of his mighty power, Which he wrought in Christ, when he raised him from the dead, and set him at his own right hand in the heavenly places. . .Now unto him that is able to do exceeding abundantly above all that we ask or think, according to the power that worketh in us."

This is the birthright or inheritance or true identity of the church; however, it is the rule rather than the exception that this identity is not manifested through the *soul* or unique personality of the church. While this identity may not be an ideal that can not be realized, as witness the first century church, we know that that church was a suffering church compared with the all too comfortable church which most of us have experienced. While it is true that persecution purifies the church that its true colors might be revealed, most of us would rather read about it than to volunteer to replicate that church in the twentieth or twenty first century!

When the church is operating in the strength of the flesh, or Self is in the ascendancy, that which is manifested through the *SOUL* or outward display, within and to the world, has been described in the State of the Church but is summarized in the 6 characteristics listed:

1. DISUNITY-There is a lack of cohesiveness within the church when everyone tends to do that which is right in his own eyes (Judges 17:6). This is not to imply that there is a state of total anarchy, but the unity given by the Holy Spirit does not necessarily accompany the majority opinion; in fact, the majority is usually wrong! As previously stated, there is usually more unity when there is a visible project or a fight against a visible enemy. The spiritual goals which are so desperately needed are not understood or given priority since the majority of the believers do not have the discernment to recognize the needs nor the commitment to give their lives toward their being realized. Frequently, those who are led of the Lord to implement spiritual ministry or goals are perceived to be 'fanatics'. Someone has said that a fanatic is anyone who is more spiritual than you are!

2. CARNALITY–One does not have to go far to find evidence of churches which are charting their own destinies, pandering to the desires of the leading members, attempting to attract and impress the world by using many of its current fads, carrying out programs in the strength of the flesh, few unbelievers won to the Lord, little or no vision for missions, and a toleration for sin, or an unwillingness to confront it. This does not necessarily mean that the preponderance of the members are living in gross sin, but it is very likely that the vast majority have not embraced the Cross in the sense of losing their lives and identities based on time/space relationships. Various writers estimate that as many as ninety percent of believers never come to know experientially their true identity in Christ.

Though carnality may be represented by those who are in active defiance of God by going their own willful way, it can just as easily be the devoted Christian doing everything he can for God but doing it in his own strength and asking God to help. Ignorance of the believer's position in Christ or that the Cross can become a reality in experience through the work of the Holy Spirit accounts for much of the defeat that is the daily lot of all too many believers.

Or, there may be blatant sin on the part of members and leadership in local churches and in Christian organizations which may capture the attention of the media, local and national, in a manner that brings reproach on the name of Christ. One brand of flesh is no better than another!

3. CONDITIONAL LOVE–Many believers who need love the most deserve it the least from a human standpoint. Those who are hurting and defeated may exhibit behavior which tends to earn them more rejection. Conversely, those who receive acceptance may be its recipients for all of the wrong reasons; namely, favoritism may be shown those who are talented or who have much to offer from a financial standpoint. God's Word has something to say about having respect of persons (James 2:3,9).

There are times that business meetings of evangelical churches make the headlines in the secular press, and they are likely to say, "See how they hate one another!" I have read newspaper accounts of the police having been called to restore order in such meetings. If we looked underneath the surface of some of the lives involved, we might have reason to say, "Blessed are the troublemakers for they are very close to coming to the end of themselves!". However, most of the faithful are too involved in the fracas to see (or, sometimes, care about) God's perspective; they are absorbed in being right and contending (and being contentious) for the faith.

4. CHURCH MEETINGS–In all too many churches, the morning service is advertised as the "Worship Service"; but precious little worship actually takes place. A preaching service can evoke worship, but the two are not necessarily synonymous. A sermon all too frequently takes the place of a message from God, and the music may be technically flawless but entertain rather than minister to the hearers.

5. ALIENATION AND FRAGMENTATION IN RELATIONSHIPS–The carnage in the wake of broken homes, damaged interpersonal relationships, church splits, grudges, addictions, etc., are all too familiar to believers inside and outside of the church. Rejection which has been sustained by the believer in the past is all to often perpetuated in his relationship with the church. Too many churches have become country clubs for the well-adjusted rather than hospitals which can minister to the needs of devastated believers or unbelievers who frequent the services.

6. PROGRAMS and perspiration often take the place of prevailing prayer. While I am not opposed to programs or organization in the body of believers, it is all too easy to devise, borrow, adapt or adopt approaches to working with people which do not have the stamp of the Holy Spirit upon them. In fact, as has been previously stated, world system developments find their way into the church with not so subtle disguises; the encroachments of psychology in its varied forms have pervaded the church on such a wide scale as to deceive even the very elect.

The *BODY* in the church as an organization, instead of an organism, is represented by the individual members and by the physical plant made of bricks and mortar which has come to be known as the church. Impressive buildings, lavish furnishings, and great productions make an appeal to the world and to the soulish desires of its members. In many churches the bodies of believers may be very comfortable in the surroundings, while the soul may not be at all uncomfortable by the placating or entertaining sermon which takes the place of a message. Success may be measured to a great extent by the numbers of people which are sitting on the premises instead of those which are standing on the promises.

THE FALL AND RISE OF THE CHURCH

The process of God's dealing with the self-centered church is depicted in the following diagram. The downward trend shows the stripping process through which the church must go to deal with that which has been produced by leaning on the arm of the flesh. Though there are times when the church is used of the Lord–spurts of spirituality–the trend is generally downward just as in the life of the individual.

When the church begins to go through the death throes, there may be convulsions which will be detrimental to all concerned. However, death to the old is an absolute necessity if the church is to begin a new life in the power of the Spirit–resurrection life reflected in revival. It is at this point that the temptation to bring on the life supports must be resisted by those who have the spiritual understanding to know what God is doing; this will, undoubtedly, be the decided minority of the membership.

The emerging new church (See Diagram 2) is shown coming out of the Cross with the personality of the new church beginning to reflect the qualities of Christ as its Life. Again, just as with the individual,

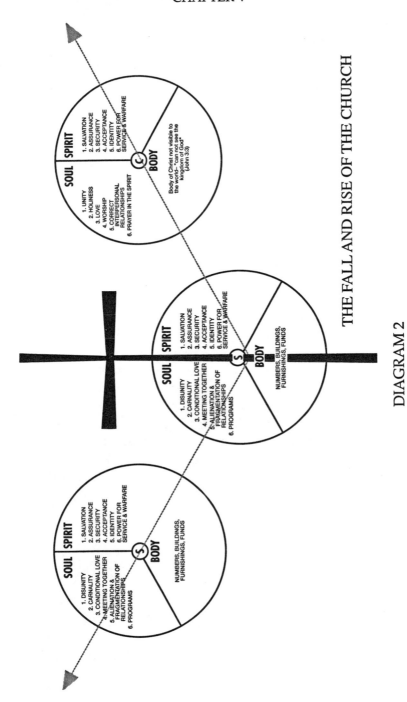

THE FALL AND RISE OF THE CHURCH

DIAGRAM 2

the changes may be gradual or there may be some sudden transformations if the Lord elects to do a crisis work in the church. If there is a mighty moving of the Holy Spirit in a short period of time the change will be evident to all. It can be just as real and just as transforming if the Holy Spirit moves slowly and surely in the life of the church.

The attributes shown in the Self-centered church may be dealt with by the Holy Spirit sovereignly as the church as a whole submits to the Lordship of Christ. The scriptures are very clear on what the church is and what God expects of His Bride. However, the flesh being what it is, the church frequently must go through suffering before it begins to respond to the wooing of the Holy Spirit, much in the same way that the individual does. In the words of Phil. 1:29,30: "For unto you it is given in the behalf of Christ, not only to believe on him, but also to suffer for his sake; Having the same conflict which ye saw in me, and now hear to be in me." I believe these words can be applied equally to the individual believer and to the corporate manifestation known as the church.

There is nothing like suffering to get our undivided attention for a prolonged period of time! Without a need, we are unlikely to make a desperate search for a supply. When everything is going well in the church, there is the tendency to coast; and we always coast downhill! Even when things seem to be going well, we are still going downhill spiritually when we are attempting to live the Christian life in our own strength; as a church, we are united in heading downward–*lost but making good time!* When all of our best efforts with our best fleshly foot forward results in continued chaos, we just *might* get the message that all is not well!

Calling flesh by its proper name when it involves

the church and church leadership, trying to be good for God, is not usually accepted with tender, loving appreciation! It is one thing to apply such nomenclature to open, flagrant sin; it is quite another to expose the carnality of dedicated self effort. There is a real premium on flesh in the church; put it on a great enough guilt trip, and you can get all kinds of work out of it! In fact, *many people will work themselves to death to keep from dying*! And churches will mortgage themselves to the hilt to keep the machinery going and keep up the appearance of success in the face of obvious failure.

Just as with the individual, *when all else fails* it is time to do it God's way. It seems that we must exhaust all of the resources of the flesh before we will accept God's assessment of the matter: "For I know that in me (that is, in my flesh,) dwelleth no good thing: for to will is present with me; but how to perform that which is good I find not." (Rom. 7:18) And on to the end of the chapter, "O wretched man (*church*) that I am! who shall deliver me (*us*) from the body of this death? I thank God through Jesus Christ our Lord. So then with the mind I myself (*we the church*) serve the law of God ; but with the flesh the law of sin." (Rom. 7:24,25) (Italicized words mine)

The bad news about the flesh ends with Romans 7, and the good news of the Spirit begins with Romans 8:1: "There is now no condemnation to them that are in Christ Jesus. . . . " Whether with the individual or the church, coming to the end signals a new beginning; after crucifixion comes the glorious resurrection! No, it is not perfection for the individual nor the congregation of individuals; but new life begets new life as revival spreads to other believers, *and even the world will go to watch a church when it is on fire*! Would that we could have a conflagration with the fire of spreading from one individual to another and from one church to another! I do not believe this is wishful thinking; but, rather, it is God's perfect will for His Bride.

SOUL
1. UNITY
2. HOLINESS
3. LOVE
4. WORSHIP
5. CORRECT INTERPERSONAL RELATIONSHIPS
6. PRAYER IN THE SPIRIT

SPIRIT
1. SALVATION
2. ASSURANCE
3. SECURITY
4. ACCEPTANCE
5. IDENTITY
6. POWER FOR SERVICE & WARFARE

(C)

BODY
Body of Christ not visible to the world– "can not see the Kingdom of God" (John 3:3)

Diagram 3 The Christ-Centered Church

Once the church has been "reckoned to be dead to sin and alive to God" (Rom. 6:11), many of the same teachings and methods listed as attempts at resuscitation which, prior to the Cross prevented the church from getting to the Cross, may be used by the Holy Spirit to great advantage in enhancing the new life. Thus, all that God has taught the members of the Body may be implemented in the power of the Spirit as the Life of Christ unfolds within the Body and the church emerges as a Christ-centered church displaying the revival and transformation that the Holy Spirit has wrought. It will be noted that the Spirit of the church is unchanged; the Spirit of God is merely bringing to pass in the personality or outward manifestation of the church that which has always been and always will be the true nature of the church triumphant!

It is to be expected that the upward trend will be marked by occasional losses or downers since Satan will now make this church #1 on his 'hit list'. This will be reflected as the re-emergence of the self-centered church which will have to be dealt with on a continual basis. Not only will the members of the Body become free and live under grace instead of law; but, also, they will be used as instruments of grace to see other believers set free, and many who are lost will come under the influence of the gospel as believers display a Christianity that works! Many believers are hesitant to witness to the lost because they do not want to export something that is not working at home.

One physician with whom I counseled was so depressed that he would send his patients to a pastor down the street to be led to the Lord since he didn't want them to get what he had! Now, however, he is able to witness to the lost and the saved and see God bring about transformation in the lives of both–*to God be the glory!*

The characteristics of the Christ-centered church are depicted in Diagram 3. It is to be understood that the revived church will not manifest all of the traits immediately, but there will be changes in enough areas that those inside and outside will begin to sit up and take notice as the Holy Spirit's presence is in evidence. There will be changes taking place that all of man's effort could not produce; transformed lives will result in transformed relationships, and believers will be set free to minister in ways never before thought possible.

It will be noted that the characteristics of the

SPIRIT of the church are unchanged from that of the Self-centered church. As with the individual believer, the church is complete–". . .a glorious church, not having spot, or wrinkle, or any such thing; but that it should be holy and without blemish." (Eph.5:27)

However, the *SOUL* or personality now reflects the work of the Holy Spirit; and *we see the Church as an organism rather than an organization.* This is not to say that there is no organization in the spiritual church, but the organization takes place as a result of what God is doing and for His glory rather than being a memorial to man's effort to accomplish man's end.

THE SOUL

We will be looking at the *SOUL* of the church in the book of Ephesians, though much could be added by referring to Paul's other letters. The first characteristic is that of

1. *UNITY* (Eph.4:1-16) out of which flows the areas in which the unity of the Spirit (Eph.4:3) will be manifested; these are: Doctrine, Virtues, Spiritual Gifts, Ministry, Edification, and Love.

Disunity is the product of pride, strife, and impatience. Unity is the product of humility, a forbearing spirit, and patience. Unity is given by the Holy Spirit; if we truly love one another with *agape* love, the Spirit, Himself, will keep the bond of peace. Paul uses the body analogy and the working of the various body parts as an illustration of the body of Christ and the individuals with their various gifts. All gifts must be used to the edifying of the body to achieve unity. Gifts used to edify the individual member will bring disunity. Paul instructs us that we are to reach a unity of faith with Christ, the perfect man, as His body being manifest on Earth. To keep our objective pure, we must speak the truth in love. When we do this, we manifest the second characteristic, that of

2. HOLINESS (Eph.4:17-32, 5:7-14).

Holiness demands that we live in stark contrast to the world. This new life style is not a matter of doing or action alone but a matter of being. The church must be filled with men who have renewed minds. But this manner of 'learning Christ' is not solely a matter of knowing truth, but also of finding truth *in Jesus*. We are to put off the former conversation of the old man; this means the actions or works of the old man. We are not instructed to put off the old man because this was already accomplished at the cross; the old man was crucified (Rom. 6:6) and put off (Col. 3:9,10). Biblical holiness is the product of the indwelling Spirit of Christ: "And that ye put on the new man, which after God is created in righteousness and true holiness." (Eph. 4:24) When the church is an organism, not an organization, then the list of affirmative actions or good works will flow from the new life of Christ and not the self-righteous works of the law. But this is summarized in a simple statement of the third characteristic,

3. LOVE (Eph. 5:2).

We are to walk or act and live in love. But this is not some sentimental, do-good, humanistic kind of love; instead, we are to manifest the kind of love that Christ has shown us. This love is *agape*, a love which is unconditional, His love. Having experienced grace, we are to show grace. Verse one of Chapter 5 commands us: "Be ye therefore followers of God, as dear children". We are to manifest a godlike character because we are the children of God. We are to act like the new creatures which we, in fact, are. This kind of life will lead to the fourth characteristic:

4. *WORSHIP* (Eph. 5:18-20):
Worship is to be an external expression of what we are internally. Just as a man filled with wine acts under its influence, so the man filled with the Spirit will act under His influence. Thankfulness, praise and singing are the outflow of a church and the people being continuously filled to overflow with the Spirit. People so controlled will manifest the fifth characteristic:

5. *CORRECT INTERPERSONAL RELATIONSHIPS* (5:21,22,25,33; 6:1,2): The marriage relationship, the family relationship, and employer/employee relationships, are all addressed under the same topic of Eph. 5:21: "Submitting yourselves one to another in the fear of God". If we seek to please Christ as He resides in the other person and if we allow Christ to live His life out in our relationships how can Christ cause a fight with Christ? As Christ lives His life out in the church, we will be moved to intercede for each other in the sixth characteristic:

6. *PRAYER IN THE SPIRIT* (6:18)
Again, we notice that prayer is to be controlled by and motivated by the indwelling Spirit. This means that we will not offer a simple and obligatory 'word of prayer'. We will be moved to intercede on behalf of all our brothers and sisters in persevering prayer. Just as the battle of Eph. 6:10-17 calls us to fight not in our own strength but in His, so also our prayers will be filled with His strength and vigor. All the actions of the individual and the church must be balanced with what Paul teaches in the earlier verses of Ephesians.

For example, Eph. 3:19,20 states: "And to know the love of Christ, which passes knowledge, that ye might be filled with all the fullness of God. Now unto Him that is able to do exceeding abundantly above all that we ask or think, according to the power that worketh in us." The church as an organism will manifest the very life of Christ to a dying world.

THE BODY

The *BODY* is to be recognized as the Body of Christ which is an organism and does not rely primarily on its physical manifestation. It is heavenly in its calling, and is oriented toward relationships in its walk. We can see the manifestation of the church through spiritual believers, but we can not see the church itself. The true church is not built of bricks and mortar, but as we read in 1 Peter 2:5,6,9: "Ye also as lively stones, are built up a spiritual house, an holy priesthood, to offer up spiritual sacrifices, acceptable to God by Jesus Christ. Wherefore also it is contained in the scripture, Behold, I lay in Sion a chief corner stone, elect, precious: and he that believeth on him shall not be confounded. But ye are a chosen generation, a royal priesthood, an holy nation, a peculiar people; that ye should shew forth the praises of him who hath called you out of darkness into his marvellous light: Which in time past were not a people, but are now the people of God: which had not obtained mercy, but now have obtained mercy."

The spiritual church will see, "What is *the exceeding greatness of his power to us-ward who believe*, according to the working of his mighty power, Which he wrought in Christ, when he raised him from the dead, and set him at his own right hand in the heavenly places. . .And hath raised us up together, and made us sit together in heavenly places in Christ Jesus:. . ." and ". . .is able to do exceeding abundantly above all that we ask or think, according to the power that worketh in us, *Unto him be glory in the church* by Christ Jesus throughout all ages, world without end. Amen." (Eph. 1:18-20, 2:6, 3:20,21)

Thus, the church will be prepared to withstand the onslaughts of the enemy as described in 6:10-13,18: "Finally, my brethren, be strong in the Lord and in the power of his might. Put on the whole armour of God, that ye may be able to stand against the wiles of the devil. For we wrestle not against flesh and blood, but against principalities, against powers, against the rulers of the darkness of this world, against spiritual wickedness in high places. Wherefore take unto you the whole armour of God, that ye may be able to withstand in the evil day, and having done all, to stand . . . Praying always with all prayer and supplication in the Spirit, and watching thereunto with all perseverance and supplication for all saints."

CHAPTER VI
A PLAN FOR EDIFYING
THE CHURCH

As you have already seen, there is nothing in what I have written that is new to the church; someone has said, "If it is new, it is not true; if it is true, it is not new." However, the truth of the experienced Cross has been all but lost in the last half of this century, beginning with the Higher Criticism of the German theologians and the liberalism which has resulted from it, in my opinion. Even in evangelical Christianity, we have all but become a 'do it yourself' religion; perhaps much of it should be called 'churchianity' instead of Christianity. While God always has His servants who preach the whole counsel of God, those faithful pastors who clearly preach the Cross in this sense are the exception rather than the rule in the church today.

I dare not suggest a new 'program', but I would like to pose a novel proposition that the church give equal emphasis to the roles of evangelism and discipleship. While some churches have well organized discipleship programs, a review of the literature extant in the various aspects of discipleship will show that most of the materials produced for use in such programs are strangely silent on the experienced Cross. It is my opinion that discipleship without the Cross is not really discipleship but a farce! Such programs may teach much about discipline and the various aspects of the Christian life which are enjoined by scripture; but, absent the Cross, the net result is that the flesh will have been strengthened– exactly the opposite result that is taught in 2 Cor. 12:9: *"And he said unto me, My grace is sufficient for thee: for my strength is made perfect in weakness. Most gladly therefore will I rather glory in my infirmities, that the power of Christ may rest upon me."* And in 2 Cor. 4:11: *"For we which live are alway delivered unto death for Jesus' sake, that the life also of Jesus might be made manifest in our mortal flesh."*

I would like to suggest a model into which the truth of the Cross may be implemented, and you will note that many churches already have some of the components in place and functioning. The model depicts the church as a Funnel into which people are introduced in various ways–visitors, transfers, the results of the evangelistic outreach, etc. To introduce this model, I would like to speak in terms of the Pulpit and the Pew.

THE PULPIT

Over our more than two decades of ministry at GFI, we have found greater acceptance by far among those believers who are hurting, whether they be in the pulpit or the pew. Since the overwhelming majority of believers occupy the pew, there is a greater population from which to draw than from those who are in the formal ministry. Too, those in the pew do not tend to be nearly as defensive since most do not have a theological reputation to protect, nor do they need the acceptance of the ecclesiastical community of professional Christians.

Though God has touched the lives of innumerable believers through the books, counseling, conferences and other outreach and training opportunities, it is difficult for the teaching to flow from the bottom up! It is estimated that a book such as *Handbook to Happiness* is read by approximately 10 people; if that is the case, almost 3,000,000 would have read that book. One can easily see the ripple effects of those who have been touched in person or through the reading of the first book or one of the subsequent books. However, if these who have had their lives transformed by the Holy Spirit through some of these helps begin to reach out with a truth that the pastor is not party to or friendly with, it can cause division within the church despite all of the intentions to the contrary. Also, such believers would not have the benefit of systematic follow-up which would serve the purpose of stabilizing them in the new walk–the walk in the Spirit (Gal. 5:16). When that follow-up is not available, there will be significant regression which causes some to doubt that the results are lasting.

Therefore, it is vital that the truth of the Cross be proclaimed from the pulpit–from the top down, through the messages and the leadership until it permeates every aspect of the life of the church. This is not to say that the pastor teaches this truth and nothing else as though he has a 'one-stringed banjo'; it *is* to say that the truth of the Cross and grace should be the flavoring for everything else that is taught from the beginning to the end of the range of doctrine.

It goes without saying that the pastor himself must have gone through the death/resurrection process or he will not be able to teach it in a way that brings life. *"So then death worketh in us, but life in you."* (2 Cor. 4:12) must be a guiding principle in his life and ministry if he is to see this truth become more than so many words to his hearers.

Most pastors will require a number of years after having experienced the liberating power of the Cross before they will be able to communicate it effectively and without causing rifts in the church. Obviously, this is not going to be the most welcome message to the flesh; and it will be just the opposite to the preaching that has been the diet of a lifetime for many, if not most, of his parishioners. It should not be surprising, then, that many will have spiritual indigestion and need some tender 'burping' here and there as they tend to choke on meat when they have been accustomed to a diet of milk. Some may even need a spiritual 'Heimlich maneuver'! In this milieu, it is a given that the whole area must be approached with spiritual sensitivity as walking where angels fear to tread.

Some pastors who have been set free through the work of the Holy Spirit in renewing their minds have assayed to set forth the truth immediately to their people only to find a personal rejection as well as rejection of the message and have had to find new churches in a very short time. The author knows of one pastor who found exactly the opposite. He approached his church with much wisdom and spiritual sensitivity and saw the Spirit of God turn the whole church around in revival in a very short time. After the church was settled in to continue the process, he was called by a smaller church in another state and saw the same receptivity on the part of another congregation. It can be done, but it must be initiated and carried out in the power of the Holy Spirit with wisdom given from above (James 1:5).

THE PEW

Once the pastor's life, his commitment to the message of the Cross, his pulpit ministry, and the church leadership have come under the influence of the Cross, he is ready to prepare the leadership of the church to

176

put in place those additional units not presently functioning, while assuring that each activity within the purview of the church has integrated within it the message of the Cross and grace. The Funnel in the diagram, the church, will direct those who come into it to a filtering process whereby each member who comes in will be evaluated to see where (s)he fits into the framework of the church.

It could be that a NEW MEMBERS' CLASS would be appropriate for new candidates for membership, and most churches have such a class already in place. Such a class should present the basics of the faith from salvation to identification, not just indoctrinate incoming members with some denominational jargon and the practices of the particular local church. This will help each candidate to evaluate his own spiritual maturity, having been given a 'spiritual yardstick' against which to compare his growth. He may find that he is psychologically well adjusted but totally out of adjustment, spiritually. If so, he may request or be pointed toward counseling for spiritual growth which, in the model, is termed, CRISIS DISCIPLESHIP.

Or, it may be that one or more of the family members express the need for help with emotional or behavioral problems. If so, crisis discipleship will take precedence over the new members' class. The coordinator of the crisis discipleship ministry should be available to consult with new candidates to make the arrangements for the necessary appointments.

This assumes that there will be a cadre of believers trained in crisis discipleship to meet the person where he is and to point him to the Cross, either for salvation, sanctification (the experienced Cross) or both. This type of ministry is normally called counseling; but, as we have described it in the Personal Spiritual Clinic, it is really spiritual ministry. Each person trained in this

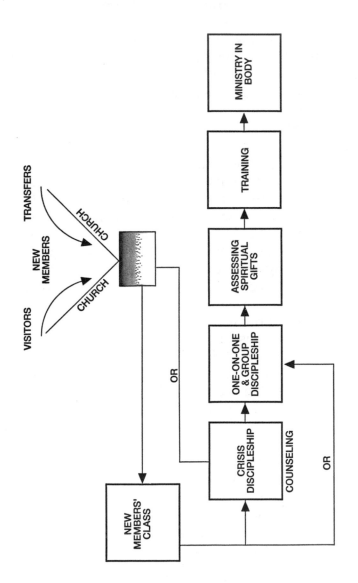

DIAGRAM 4: A SUGGESTED MODEL FOR IMPLEMENTATION

type of ministry could see 3 people one night each week until each finds victory.

If it is determined that the person is not born again, the way of salvation from the scriptures may be augmented by the use of the *Line Diagram* and/or the new tract by GFI, *How to Have a Life of Freedom*, that the prospect may understand both aspects of the Cross at the same time. It is a travesty on the gospel to separate the Blood Jesus shed on the Cross for forgiveness of the sins of the lost person, from the work of the Cross to bring death to the old life (old man) and pave the way for the Holy Spirit's regenerating work, thus putting on the new man (Colossians 3:9,10). It is just such separation, or giving half of the gospel, that results in the new believer's understanding the half of the gospel that brings forgiveness but not the half that brings victory! When new believers are given the whole gospel, there will be reduced need for the remedial steps for the church which have been the focus of this entire book. Poor evangelism or an incomplete gospel has been responsible for much of the predicament in which we find ourselves at this juncture in the life of the church.

The *Line Diagram* has proven to be a very effective tool for evangelism. This being the case, it is not necessary to shift gears when continuing the process of discipleship; the whole of salvation from start to finish may be taught using this simple diagram. The old adage certainly applies here, "*An ounce of prevention is worth a pound of cure!*" (It is anticipated that GFI will shortly produce a new book, *Handbook to Happiness in Evangelism* by the author and Dr. C. R. Bailey, GFI Missions Director, which incorporates the teaching herein advocated.)

The Holy Spirit has honored the use of the *Wheel and Line* presentation over the past 22 years, and this is the backbone of the teaching which is being suggested–both at the entry level (evangelism) and in the ongoing discipleship. The aforementioned book will make maximum advantage of this material and the experience gained since the inception of the ministry. We have seen those with an 8th grade education be mightily used of God in teaching the Cross in this manner, and lives have been radically transformed by the Holy Spirit. The book, *Counseling with the Mind of Christ*, details the use of the Wheel and Line in the one-on-one relationship in detail in Chapter 5. The study material in the Personal Spiritual Clinic not only enables you to assimilate the truth, but it can be used verbatim in sharing with another.

As you can readily see, the use of the *Wheel and Line* (also available in tract form for personal work) with a believer is very much akin to sharing the way of salvation with the lost. The sinner, having been prepared by the Holy Spirit through conviction of sin, is led to Christ and the Holy Spirit gives new birth. Similarly, the saint who has been prepared by the Holy Spirit through conviction of the flesh and concomitant suffering of brokenness, is led to the Cross and the Holy Spirit brings revival into the soul of the believer. With the sinner, it is important not to get tangled up in all of the details of his life of sin and in the smoke screen questions that he brings up to avoid facing his lost condition; it is most important that he sees his true condition as lost and undone before a holy God. Once the Holy Spirit has registered this in his heart, he is ready to place his trust in the Lord Jesus Christ as his Lord and Savior.

Similarly, it is important not to get tangled up in all of the psychological and social conflict in which a believer finds himself, or it will not be possible to see the woods for the trees! Understanding the person's pain and situation is necessary, but the primary objective is for the believer to see that it is not these symptoms that are the real issue; it is the *flesh* or *self-centered* life that is paramount and which must be dealt with by the Cross. Once the Holy Spirit has brought this home to him and he is willing to lose his life in order to save it (John 12:24,25, Matthew 16:24,25), he can pray a "selfer's prayer" much as the sinner prays a "sinner's prayer"; we can expect God on the basis of His revealed Word to transform the life by renewing his mind just as He said! Such a transformation may be gradual or in a crisis as is described in *Handbook to Happiness* and *Ins and Out of Rejection*.

Once the Holy Spirit has done the needed work in the life and the believer is levelled out in the new walk, he may be turned over to a discipleship unit for ONE-ON-ONE AND GROUP DISCIPLESHIP for a period of up to a year. The discipler in the crisis unit may pick up another person and take them through the same teaching .

The overarching purpose of discipleship is to see that the Cross is applied in every area of the believer's life. Though he has entered into victory by reckoning himself to be dead to sin and alive unto God (Rom. 6:11), this must become a daily (Lk. 9:23) and continuous (2 Cor. 4:11) faith transaction. It is not an isolated experience (if it *is* an experience) that results in continuous victory forever thereafter; nor does it result in sinless perfection. Also, instruction must be given that will warn the believer against passivity. Especially, those who have been steeped in legalism may have a tendency to pull back from what may have been a bee hive of activity in attempting to live the Christian life. Counseling toward a balance between obedience and grace is a must in the early days of discipleship. An overemphasis on grace at the expense of obedience can result in passivity or license; emphasizing obedience at the expense of grace will result in legalism. One is as bad as the other since both will produce an unbalanced Christian life.

There are many excellent materials which may be used in this phase of the discipleship process; however, it will be necessary to integrate the Cross in much of the existing material. The crying need is not for more materials or tools but for believers who have experienced the Cross in their own lives and are willing to 'get involved' in the lives of others over an extended period of time. To use the terminology of the market place, this ministry will be *labor intensive.* In other words, there will be a proportionately larger number of people involved in the process who will require training and supervision. Also, those who are vitally involved in discipling others are likely to be unsung heroes! Evangelism produces tangible results much more quickly, and there is more widespread understanding of the activity. Discipleship pays great dividends in the long haul but requires much patience and endurance.

Mr. Theron Messer, executive vice-president of GFI, and myself are planning to co-author a book to be used for followup, which will help to pull together existing materials along with integrating the concepts suggested in this book. The books authored by Dr. Harold Burchett (See Appendix A) will be found helpful in all phases of church life, but particularly in the area of discipleship.

After the period of formal discipleship is over, the believer should be assisted in ASSESSING HIS SPIRITUAL GIFTS and the type of ministry that would be suitable for his gifts and experience. Then, it is necessary that he be placed under teaching and/or on-the-job training that will be conducive to his development along the lines that God has gifted him and where the Holy Spirit will anoint his ministry. Once he is so equipped, he can be placed into the ministry of the body and not be a square peg in a round hole or be thrust prematurely into ministry for which he is unprepared spiritually or by way of training.

There will be those who come under the influence of the church who will have been prepared elsewhere and who have gifts already honed for use in the body; these could be placed immediately in the proper place of service for which they have been prepared of the Lord, both by experience and training.

PREPARATION OF LEADERSHIP

Implementation of the preaching and teaching of the Cross will necessitate that a group of believers undergo some intensive training to be in the forefront as others are brought to the understanding of who they are in Christ. Over the years, we have found that a conference of 8-10 hours is sufficient to teach the basic content and introduce the concept of discipleship and ministry to the entire church.

This is followed by a workshop where the attendees are placed in triads, or groups of three, where they practice on each other in sharing the truths learned in the conference, primarily in the form of the *Wheel and Line*. This 'hands on' training forces the participant to interact with the material or truth and see where he is in the death/resurrection process as well as learning to communicate it to others. It is in this setting that many have found the reality of the Cross as the Holy Spirit ministers to them, frequently through another novice who is learning to share the truth of the Cross for the first time.

The material contained in the Personal Spiritual Clinic in conjunction with my other books and, possibly, my entire conference on video tape will enable the believer or a group to study and participate in training which will result in individual victory or revival and the ability to lead others into that same victory. Out of such a workshop will come a number of believers who are desirous of learning, over a period of time, to be effective in sharing not only the gospel with the lost but, also, with the saved. It is likely that God will raise up a person from this training that will be His choice servant to train others in the body.

Such a training program has been implemented by several churches at this writing with more in the process. Two of the early programs were at Church of Glad Tidings in Austin, TX and First Baptist of Atlanta. As training proceeded in the Austin church, there were those who surfaced who were extremely gifted in working with particular populations; some worked with victims of sexual abuse, others with marriages, others with those involved in substance abuse, others with adolescents, etc. First Baptist of Atlanta has an ongoing training program for lay counselors which is well organized and disciplined and has been proven in the furnace of affliction.

Other churches have implemented the teaching using the materials in unique ways. A church near St. Paul, MN used the *Wheel and Line* as the foundation or cornerstone of its discipleship program to great advantage. GFI staff is available for consultation in establishing such programs as well as putting you in touch with churches and pastors who have put their shoulders to the wheel (no pun intended) and can be of encouragement to those launching a New Testament discipleship program.

CHAPTER VII
A CHALLENGE
TO THE CHURCH

It is in knowing who we are, whose we are, loving and committing to one another that the union of believers known as the Body of Christ might be a challenge to a fragmented and alien society–that the world again might say, "See how they love one another!" Individualistic Christianity may no longer be an option, and it never was scriptural. Survival in this world could well depend upon that cohesive bond among believers.

In the early settlement of this country, the believers were in an alien environment where they suffered privation on every hand. In addition to building homes and trying to find provision of food, there was the ever present danger of being slaughtered by Native Americans who were then called Indians. Their very survival depended upon their covenant relationship with each other and their close walk with God. When either of these relationships was in disrepair, there was the likelihood of failure in their proposed establishment of one nation under God, or establishment of a nation, period. Those who were most vital in the leadership were not the politicians or military geniuses but men of God such as Jonathan Edwards, Cotton Mather, Increase Mather and others of the Puritan preachers who were able to unite the people under God for whatever sacrifice was required for the common good.

The enemies we are facing today are just as formidable but not as recognizable to the untrained eye; the humanists and New Age devotees have not yet come after believers with scalping in view, but many are advocating a violent end for Christians to pave the way for their new world order. Humanism in its varied forms, such as New Age teaching, has engulfed us and has invaded all of our institutions, with the church not having escaped unscathed. We have looked at many of the ways in which the church has imbibed of the fragrance of the world system rather than counting itself crucified to the world (Galatians 6:14). The admonition of scripture to be separate from the world has never been more timely: "Wherefore, come out from among them, and be ye separate, saith the Lord, and touch not the unclean thing; and I will receive you, And will be a Father unto you, and ye shall be my sons and daughters, saith the Lord Almighty (2 Cor. 6:17,18).

Someone has aptly said, "All that is necessary for evil to thrive is for good men to do nothing." All that one has to do is to look around in our country and see that evil is winning big time! The country is all but being given over to a reprobate mind. We could back off and condemn all of those miserable sinners who are doing all of the ungodly things and making life so miserable for us (poor us!); or we can take inventory of our own lives and churches and see if we, as a church, have been guilty of 'doing nothing' which has given ground to Satan to entrench his forces.

We have tried battles with bullets, both inside and outside the country; and we have fought the battle unsuccessfully with ballots; in fact, we often elect the enemy to office! I am not saying that believers should not be active in the political process; I *am* saying it will never get us out of the mess we are in. It is a spiritual battle, as my friend Bob Dugan said, for the soul of America. As such, it will never be won with carnal weapons used in the strength of the flesh by politicians, or by ministers for that matter. "For the weapons of our warfare are not carnal but mighty through God to the pulling down of strongholds. . . .(2 Cor. 10:4). . . "Not by might, nor by power, but by my spirit, saith the Lord of hosts" (Zech. 4:6).

I would like for us to look at our country in much the same way we have been looking at our individual lives and the church. The individual believer too often relies on the strength of the flesh, even purchased flesh such as therapy, when the chips are down and assistance must be obtained. Likewise, the church turns to programs, prestige, and professionals to bolster its sagging flesh and put some Band-Aids on the cancer which is eating away at its vital organs. Should we then condemn the secular society which has no other way to turn; or, should we get biblical about this whole thing and see that judgment begins at the house of God? If we do not judge ourselves, we can rest assured that God will judge us and that certain chastisement will take place. Hebrews 12 describes the chastisement of the individual believer that he might be a partaker of God's holiness. Why should we not expect, then, that God will apply this same principle to His people corporately?

As individuals, we can understand from the scriptures God's plan to deal with our flesh, or selfishness, and cooperate with Him as He reveals the truth of our union with Christ and sets us free from ourselves. Likewise, we can have the discernment given by the Holy Spirit as to the chastisement that God allows in our churches to bring them to the end of themselves. Whether as individuals or churches, cooperation with the Holy Spirit softens and shortens the process; going our own willful way and doing our own thing, individually or corporately, will guarantee more suffering and a lengthy process, and everyone within and without loses in the process. The longer we bow our necks against God in our service with dedicated flesh, the longer it will be before our churches can be a part of the answer instead of part of the problem.

Just as we extrapolated from the individual to the church in God's dealing with the flesh, I do not think it is without scriptural foundation that our entire nation can be humbled and brought to the end of itself in similar fashion. God dealt with Israel through its enemies many times, and He does not love us any less than He did them! Therefore, it is going to have to be the spirit of the nation (the church) that guides the way if the soul of the nation is to be 'saved'. However, if the church is yet operating in the strength of the flesh, it is going to give an uncertain sound in attempting to lead the nation out of the Wilderness into the Promised Land. It is very difficult to lead someone to a place that you have not been; it is almost as difficult as trying to come back from a place that you have not gone!

I am afraid that, individually and corporately, we want to have the benefits of resurrection life without the suffering of the Cross. I do not enjoy suffering any more than anyone else; a person would have to be a masochist to elect suffering for the sake of suffering. However, the suffering in view here has a purpose just as we see in Hebrews 12:2: "Looking unto Jesus the author and finisher of our faith; who for the joy that was set before him endured the cross, despising the shame, and is set down at the right hand of the throne of God." We can not escape the suffering of the Cross if we are to know the power of His resurrection: "That

I may know him, and the power of his resurrection, and the fellowship of his sufferings, being made conformable unto his death" (Phil. 3:10). And in Phil. 1; 29,30 we read: "For unto you it is given in the behalf of Christ, not only to believe on him, but also to suffer for his sake; Having the same conflict which ye saw in me, and now hear to be in me."

It is always easier to be a Monday morning quarterback and criticize that which is being done than to get in the harness and lead the way. We can formulate what we would like the church to be and point out all of its shortcomings. However, God is calling each of us to personal revival that we, in turn, might be instruments of revival in our homes, churches and nation; and the only way we can do that is for God to get us out of the way through the experienced Cross. It is not glamorous and exciting; it is the way of suffering, humiliation and death. Most of us would rather push others to the Cross ahead of us than to lead the way in sacrifice; suffering and deprivation are not the favorite pastimes of any sane person. The church is made up of individuals, and we must go to the Cross one by one if the church is to be revived and renewed. "Then said Jesus unto his disciples, If any man will come after me, let him deny himself, and take up his cross, and follow me. For whosoever will save his life shall lose it: and whosoever will lose his life for my sake shall find it" (Matt. 16:24,25).

I am firmly convinced that the church must be revived if our nation is to have the leadership it needs and if it is to be a light in the consuming darkness that is coming upon the face of the world. Will you join me in prayer for the churches in this country that the message of the Cross might be the theme that will unite believers in spiritual fellowship, despite denominational lines and petty sectarian biases? As revival is communicated one-on-one, family to family and church to church, we can expect the Holy Spirit to empower the witness of believers to the lost and see the church revealed as the Body of Christ that the gates of Hell shall not be able to prevail against it. God *will* send revival if we are ready to lose our lives that He might live *His* in power and great victory; then, the world will know that the Lord Jesus Christ is the Way, the Truth and the Life (Jn. 14:6). "Now thanks be unto God, which always causeth us to triumph in Christ, and maketh manifest the savour of his knowledge by us in every place." (2 Cor. 2:14)

We are informed in John 12:24-26: "Verily, verily, I say unto you, Except a corn of wheat fall into the ground and die, it abideth alone: but if it die, it bringeth forth much fruit. He that loveth his life shall lose it; and he that hateth his life in this world shall keep it unto life eternal. *If any man serve me, let him follow me*: and where I am, there shall also my servant be; if any man serve me, him will my Father honour."

In obeying His command to serve him, we must follow Him to and through the Cross and into heavenly places if we are to abide in Him and produce much fruit (John 15:5). "If ye abide in me, and my words abide in you, ye shall ask what ye will, and it shall be done unto you (John 15:7).

"Now unto him that is able to keep you from falling, and to present you faultless before the presence of his glory with exceeding joy, to the only wise God our Saviour, be glory and majesty, dominion and power, both now and ever. Amen". (Jude 24)

I would like to end the book with a poem from my book, *Handbook to Happiness in Verse* (1988), entitled, *The Precious Blood* and a short article by A. W. Tozer. Dr. Tozer's article appeared in a book, *The Best of Tozer*, and in tract form entitled *The Old Cross and the New* published by Christian Publications, Inc., Camp Hill, PA 17011 and is used by permission. It says more in fewer words than I have found any place except in scripture and summarizes the message I have been attempting to convey in this part of the book. I trust God will challenge your heart with these words from our late brother as He did mine. Please read it prayerfully.

THE OLD CROSS AND THE NEW

"All unannounced and mostly undetected there has come in modern times a new cross into popular evangelical circles. It is like the old cross, but different: the likenesses are superficial; the differences, fundamental.

From this new cross has sprung a new philosophy of the Christian life, and from that new philosophy has come a new evangelical technique–a new type of meeting and a new kind of preaching. This new evangelism employs the same language as the old, but its content is not the same and its emphasis not as before.

The old cross would have no truck with the world. For Adam's proud flesh it meant the end of the journey. It carried into effect the sentence imposed by the law of Sinai. The new cross is not opposed to the human race; rather, it is a friendly pal and, if understood aright, it is the source of oceans of good clean fun and innocent enjoyment. It lets Adam live without interference. His life motivation is unchanged;

he still lives for his own pleasure, only now he takes delight in singing choruses and watching religious movies instead of singing bawdy songs and drinking hard liquor. The accent is still on enjoyment, though the fun is now on a higher plane morally if not intellectually.

The new cross encourages a new and entirely different evangelistic approach. The evangelist does not demand abnegation of the old life before a new life can be received. He preaches not contrasts but similarities. He seeks to key into public interest by showing that Christianity makes no unpleasant demands; rather, it offers the same thing the world does, only on a higher level. Whatever the sin-mad world happens to be clamoring after at the moment is cleverly shown to be the very thing the gospel offers, only the religious product is better.

The new cross does not slay the sinner; it redirects him. It gears him into a cleaner and jollier way of living and saves his self-respect. To the self-assertive it says, "Come and assert yourself for Christ." To the egotist it says, "Come and do your boasting in the Lord." To the thrill seeker it says, "Come and enjoy the thrill of Christian fellowship." The Christian message is slanted in the direction of the current vogue in order to make it acceptable to the public.

The philosophy back of this kind of thing may be sincere, but its sincerity does not save it from being false. It is false because it is blind. It misses completely the whole meaning of the cross.

The old cross is a symbol of death. It stands for the abrupt, violent end of a human being. The man in Roman times who took up his cross and started down the road had already said good-by to his friends. He was not coming back. He was not going out to have his life redirected; he was going out to have it ended.

194

The cross made no compromise, modified nothing, spared nothing; it slew all of the man, completely and for good. It did not try to keep on good terms with its victim. It struck cruel and hard, and when it had finished its work, the man was no more.

The race of Adam is under death sentence. There is no commutation and no escape. God cannot approve any of the fruits of sin, however innocent they may appear or beautiful to the eyes of men. God salvages the individual by liquidating him and then raising him again to newness of life.

That evangelism which draws friendly parallels between the ways of God and the ways of men is false to the Bible and cruel to the souls of its hearers. The faith of Christ does not parallel the world; it intersects it. In coming to Christ we do not bring our old life up onto a higher plane; we leave it at the cross. The corn of wheat must fall into the ground and die.

We who preach the gospel must not think of ourselves as public relations agents sent to establish good will between Christ and the world. We must not imagine ourselves commissioned to make Christ acceptable to big business, the press, or the world of sports, or modern education. We are not diplomats but prophets, and our message is not a compromise but an ultimatum.

God offers life, but not an improved old life. The life he offers is life out of death. It stands always on the far side of the cross. Whoever would possess it must pass under the rod. He must repudiate himself and concur in God's just sentence against him.

What does this mean to the individual, the condemned man who would find life in Christ Jesus? How can this theology be translated into life? Simply, he must repent and believe. He must forsake his sins and then go on to forsake himself. Let him cover nothing, defend nothing, excuse nothing. Let him not seek to make terms with God, but let him bow his head before the stroke of God's stern displeasure and acknowledge himself worthy to die.

Having done this let him gaze with simple trust upon the risen Saviour, and from Him will come life and rebirth and cleansing and power. The cross that ended the earthly life of Jesus now puts an end to the sinner; and the power that raised Christ from the dead now raises him to a new life along with Christ.

To any who may object to this or count it merely a narrow and private view of truth, let me say God has set His hallmark of approval upon this message from Paul's day to the present. Whether stated in these exact words or not, this has been the content of all preaching that has brought life and power to the world through the centuries. The mystics, the reformers, the revivalists have put their emphasis here, and signs and wonders and mighty operations of the Holy Ghost gave witness to God's approval.

Dare we, the heirs of such a legacy of power, tamper with the truth? Dare we with our stubby pencils erase the lines of the blueprint or alter the pattern shown us in the Mount? May God forbid. Let us preach the old cross and we will know the old power."

"The heart that learns to die with Christ soon knows the blessed experience of rising with Him, and all the world's persecutions cannot still the high note of holy joy that springs up in the soul that has become the dwelling place of the Holy Spirit." A.W.T.

THE PRECIOUS BLOOD

God's Word is filled with Blood
From beginning to the end–
From that of Abel's sacrifice (Gen. 4:4)
Until God His Son did send (Rom. 5:8).
In Heaven, too, its work was done (Heb. 9:23)
By Jesus, our High Priest;
In Revelation John declares,
Its power has never ceased. (Rev. 12:11)

In our finite way of thinking
We are most concerned with sins;
An confess them all we must (1 Jn. 1:9)
That Calv'ry our pardon wins.
But there is a deeper meaning
As many of us are sensing;
It goes beyond forgiveness
That, too, we might know cleansing.

Redemption has many facets,
But at Calvary it was finished; (Jn. 19:30)
Though His Blood was shed but once,
Its power is undiminished.
Through its power our Lord was raised (Heb. 13:20)
And to His Father did ascend;
His body broken at the Cross, (1 Pet. 2:24)
And the temple's veil did rend. (Matt. 27:51)

By His own Blood He entered (Heb. 9:12)
Once for all the Holy Place;
He op'ed the Fount of Blessing
Bids us to the Throne of Grace. (Heb. 4:16)
His Blood is our only merit (Heb. 10:19)
As we would His bidding do;
Our access to the Holy Place
Means our flesh we must eschew. (Lk. 9:23)

In that blessed Holy Place (Eph. 1:3)
Our life's hid with Christ in God; (Col. 3:3)
Our High Priest He can be
Because He has, likewise, trod. (Heb. 4:15)
And, so, the work in Heaven
Leaves nothing to be done,
But for us to act in faith
On the victory He has won!

As we walk with Him in light (1 Jn. 1:7)
His blood cleanses from all sin;
With others we have fellowship (1 Jn. 1:3)
As the Savior reigns within.
Cleansed from all unrighteousness (1 Jn. 1:9)
As in Christ Jesus we abide, (Jn. 15:5)
His Blood not only cleanses;
But by it we're sanctified! (Heb. 10:29,13:12)

We can know all sins are gone
And, yet, be conscience smitten;
But, again, the Blood's the answer
As in the Book 'tis written:
How much more the Blood of Christ
Through the eternal Spirit offered,
Purge your conscience from dead works–(Heb. 9:14)
The promise which is proffered.

The Blood sufficed in Heaven
Our sins with which to deal;
The Holy Spirit lacks no power,
Our sin wounds here to heal.
Our High Priest did in Heav'n
What our Mediator does on Earth; (Heb. 8:6,9:15)
Our sins completely covered *there*–
He assures us *here* our worth.

Oh, the precious Blood of Jesus
God imbued with matchless power;
That we, His sons, need not let
Sin's reign to cause us cower.
When the devil would come in
And deluge us like a flood, (Isa. 59:19)
We have only to remind him
He was conquered by the Blood.

And now, my friend, I bid you
To consider the above;
Allow the Spirit teach you
About the Fountain of His love.
His Blood covers and cleanses–
Flowing from His riven side;
But is only fraught with power
As in Christ Jesus we abide. (Jn. 15:5)

When we fail to give the Blood
Its place in our lives today,
We've all but trodden under foot (Heb. 10:29)
The Power that fills our way.
But God in sovereign grace
Continues to draw us ever;
Our lives redeemed by Precious Blood
From Him can nothing sever! (Rom. 8:38,39)

Because redemption is complete
We and our Lord know union;
'Tis in the blessed Holy Place (Heb. 9:24)
That we can know communion.
When we cease from our own works (Heb. 4:9-11)
In Him we are truly blessed;
And rejoice to do His bidding–
"Come unto me and rest." (Matt. 11:28)

C. R. Solomon

SUGGESTIONS FOR ADDITIONAL STUDY

Some of the following books will only be found in Bible school or seminary libraries since they are out of print. It seems that books on losing your life are not nearly as popular as the self-help books which tell you how you can do it, many of which fill the shelves of bookstores. However, it may be extremely profitable for you to make the trek to the library to fellowship with some of the saints of past years through their writings.

DEVOTIONAL

Boa, Ken and Max Anders	Drawing Near
Chambers, Oswald	My Utmost for His Highest
Lawrence, Brother	Practicing the Presence of God
Murray, Andrew	God's Best Secrets
Needham, David	Close to His Majesty

PRAYER

Bounds, E. M.	Power Through Prayer
Gordon, S. D.	Quiet Talks on Prayer
Guyon, Madame	Experiencing the Depths of Jesus Christ
Murray, Andrew	The Prayer Life
Taylor, Jack	Prayer, Life's Limitless Reach
Unknown Christian	Kneeling Christian

VICTORIOUS LIFE/UNION WITH CHRIST

Anderson, Neil	Victory Over the Darkness
An Unknown Christian	How to Live the Victorious Life
Burchett, Harold	Healing for the Church
(Available through GFI)	People Helping People
	Spiritual Life Studies

Cooke, Joseph R.	Free for the Taking–The Life-Changing Power of Grace
George, Bob	Classic Christianity
Gillham, Bill	Lifetime Guarantee
Gordon, S. D.	Quiet Talks on Power
Harrison, Norman B.	New Testament Living
Hession, Roy	Calvary Road
Huegel, F. J.	Bone of His Bone
Johnson, David (VanVonderen, Jeff)	The Subtle Power of Spiritual Abuse
Kazee, Buell H.	Faith is the Victory
Kuykendall, David	Our Oneness with Christ Here's Life
Legters, L. L.	The Filling of the Spirit
Lloyd-Jones, Martyn	The Cross
Lutzer, Erwin	Failure, Back Door to Success. How in This World Can I Be Holy?
MacArthur, John	The Sufficiency of Christ
Matthews, Victor	Growth in Grace
Maxwell, L. E.	Crowded to Christ Born Crucified
McConkey, James	Three-Fold Secret of the Holy Spirit
McGrath, Allister E.	The Mystery of the Cross
Meyer, F. B.	The Christ Life for Your Life The 5 "Musts" of the Christian Life
Murray, Andrew	Abide in Christ The Two Covenants Absolute Surrender
Nee, Watchman	Normal Christian Life Release of the Spirit Changed into His Likeness
Needham, David	Birthright

Palau, Luis	Say Yes! How to Renew Your Spiritual Passion
Paxson, Ruth	Life on the Highest Plane
Penn-Lewis, Jesse	The Centrality of the Cross
Pierson, A. T.	In Christ Jesus
Redpath, Alan	Victorious Christian Living
Simpson, A. B.	The Christ Life
Smith, Hannah Whitall	The Christian's Secret of a Happy Life
Solomon, Charles R.	Counseling with the Mind of Christ
	Gems and Jargon
	Handbook to Happiness
	Handbook to Happiness in Verse
	The Ins and Out of Rejection
	The Rejection Syndrome
Stanford, Miles	Green Letters
Stanley, Charles	Adversity
Stedman, Ray	Authentic Christianity
Stott, John	The Cross of Christ
Swindoll, Charles	The Grace Awakening
Taylor, Jack	Key to Triumphant Living
Thomas, Ian	The Saving Life of Christ
	The Mystery of Godliness
Tozer, A. W. (Tyndale)	That Incredible Christian
Trumbull, Charles	Victory in Christ
VanVonderen, Jeff	Tired of Trying to Measure Up
Wallis, Reginald	The New Life
Wells, Michael	Sidetracked in the Wilderness

REVIVAL

Green, Michael	Evangelism in the Early Church
Lovelace, Richard F.	1. Dynamics of Spiritual Life: An Evangelical Survey of Renewal
	2. Renewal as a Way of Life

RENEWAL

Orr, J. Edwin	The Eager Feet: Evangelical Awakenings 1790-1830
Ravenhill, Leonard	Why Revival Tarries

SPIRITUAL WARFARE

Anderson, Neil	The Bondage Breaker
Bubeck, Mark	The Adversary
Huegel, F. J.	The Mystery of Iniquity
Unger, Merrill	Demons in the World Today

BIOGRAPHIES

Fraser, J. O.	Beyond the Ranges
Hession, Roy	My Calvary Road
Taylor, Dr. and Mrs. Howard	Hudson Taylor's Spiritual Secret
Upham, Thomas C.	The Life of Madame Guyon

COMMENTARIES

Haldane, Robert	An Exposition of Romans
Harrison, Norman B.	His Salvation (Romans)
Hession, Roy	From Shadow to Substance (Hebrews)
Lloyd-Jones, D. Martyn	Romans
Moule, Charles F.D.	Christ is All (Romans, Ephesians, Colossians)
Murray, Andrew	The Holiest of All (Hebrews)
Murray, John	Romans
Newell, William R.	Romans Verse by Verse
Paxson, Ruth	The Walk, Wealth, and Warfare of the Believer
Stanley, Charles (England)	Notes on Romans

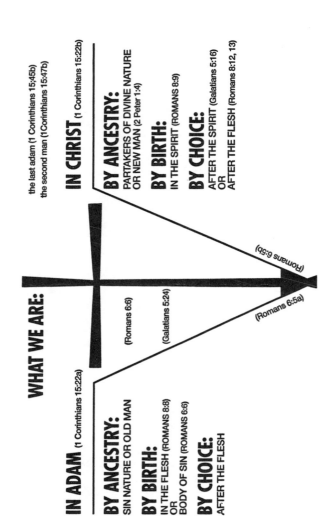

WHAT WE ARE:

IN CHRIST (1 Corinthians 15:22b)

the last adam (1 Corinthians 15:45b)
the second man (1 Corinthians 15:47b)

BY ANCESTRY:
PARTAKERS OF DIVINE NATURE
OR NEW MAN (2 Peter 1:4)

BY BIRTH:
IN THE SPIRIT (ROMANS 8:9)

BY CHOICE:
AFTER THE SPIRIT (Galatians 5:16)
OR
AFTER THE FLESH (Romans 8:12, 13)

(Romans 6:5b)

(Romans 6:6)

(Galatians 5:24)

(Romans 6:5a)

IN ADAM (1 Corinthians 15:22a)

BY ANCESTRY:
SIN NATURE OR OLD MAN

BY BIRTH:
IN THE FLESH (ROMANS 8:8)
OR
BODY OF SIN (ROMANS 6:6)

BY CHOICE:
AFTER THE FLESH

IDENTITY: WHAT WE ARE IN ADAM AND IN CHRIST

207

A SIMPLIFIED MODEL OF MAN

NATURAL OR UNREGENERATED MAN

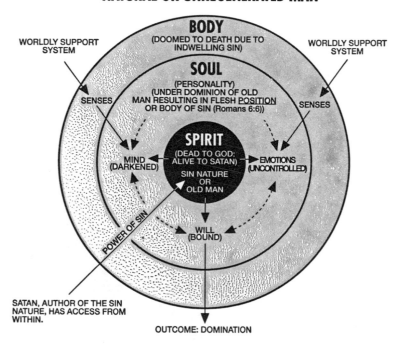

CARNAL OR FLESHLY MAN

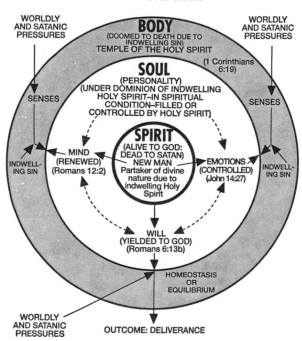

SPIRITUAL MAN

RESOURCE MATERIALS

Having pioneered a Christ-centered approach to counseling known as Spirituotherapy®, the first stage of God's mandate to GFI has been completed. Counseling and training of others, nationally and internationally, have been implemented with God's blessing. Other ministries have been established, directly and indirectly; and the books and other media are available for use in the church. Conferences, seminars, workshops, etc., may be scheduled in person or via video tape.

GFI has not granted authority to other ministries to disseminate materials of GFI origin, or cloned materials, unless a contractual relationship or permission has been secured. Marketing of tapes based on copyrighted material must also be done under contract. The fact that a ministry may have 'Grace Fellowship' in its name does not, in itself, indicate affiliation with GFI. In accordance with copyright law, reproduction and distribution of such material must have the written permission of the publisher and/or copyright owner. These restrictions are not meant in any way to discourage the sharing of the message of the cross. Certain restrictions are necessary to guard the purity of the message and to avoid violations of copyright law that we may follow the biblical mandate of 1 Cor. 14:40, "Let all things be done decently and in order."

The conferences, workshops, and other training authorized by GFI will use materials consistent with Dr. Solomon's books.

SUPPORT

GFI is a faith ministry with all gifts being tax deductible. Since the organization was decentralized in 1986, it is necessary that those desiring to support the ministry and mission of Dr. Solomon address all gifts to Grace Fellowship International, P. O. Box 27315, Denver, CO 80227. The staff of GFI must be supported primarily by gifts since many of those in need of help are not able to assist with the expense of operating the ministry.

MISSION

GFI is now making a concerted effort to use the materials and expertise developed over the last 22 years in strengthening evangelism/discipleship and indigenous missions. Teaching the message of the Cross to new believers will drastically reduce the demand for remedial counseling in whatever country.

Since the Holy Spirit is the One Who changes lives, short term missions have proven very effective in planting new works. Those desiring to help spread the message of revival in collaboration with GFI should study all of Dr. Solomon's books and avail themselves of the basic training. Contributions to such missions or mission projects may be sent to the address above. Present mission works are in Argentina and India, with fledgling works having been begun in Nigeria and Malawi. Brothers in Tanzania and Kenya have written expressing the desire for training to work in cooperation with us.

The *Wheel and Line* tract has been published in 11 languages, and *Handbook to Happiness* has been published in Spanish and Korean. Although the tract is in Russian, there is a desperate need for a composite book to be used in the training of Russian pastors, as well as major quantities of the tracts.

Dr. Solomon, Mr. Messer and Dr. Bailey are available for a variety of conferences based on the materials and/or concepts developed by GFI.

PURCHASE OF MATERIALS

All of Dr. Solomon's books and related GFI materials may be procured directly from GFI. GFI has no other trade name under which materials are sold; all orders are processed at the above address, or at the present street address (as of 1991) which is 3595 S. Teller #408, Denver, CO 80235. Quantity discounts are available as are wholesale discounts to bookstores. Those desiring to utilize conference and workshop materials may apply to GFI for affiliate status–either individual, organization or church.

Savings may be obtained by purchasing a complete set of books or a combination of books and tapes. Please send a self-addressed, stamped envelope for an order blank and price list; of course, prices are subject to change without notice. Orders may be placed by telephone, (303) 980-0003 or FAX (303) 980-1906.

MATERIALS LIST
BOOKS

Handbook to Happiness   Charles R. Solomon
Handbook to Happiness in Verse
The Ins and Out of Rejection
The Rejection Syndrome
Counseling with the Mind of Christ
(GFI has all remaining copies)
Gems and Jargon
Handbook to Happiness and You–A Spiritual Clinic

GFI conference on video tape (Dr. Solomon)
GFI conference on audio tape (Dr. Solomon)

Conference and Workshop materials;
contact us for information on affiliate status.

The Wheel and Line Tract
How to Have a Life of Freedom–GFI tract for evangelism

Caraway St. and Master's Mansion–Children's church and junior church time programs, respectively, by Ron Solomon based on the concepts in this book. (I do the remedial; Ron does the preventive!) Send a self-addressed, stamped envelope for information.

New Releases (First half of 1992)
Handbook to Happiness in Evangelism (Dr. C.R. Bailey and Dr. Charles R. Solomon)
Handbook to Happiness in Discipleship (Theron Messer and Dr. Charles R. Solomon)